T0354839

At Heaven's Door

*A Bible Study to a
Christian's Heavenly Call
from Life to Life.*

David R. Rosen

WESTBOW
PRESS®
A DIVISION OF THOMAS NELSON
& ZONDERVAN

Presented Through the Remembrance
of My Beloved Wife, Sandy

WestBow Press books may be ordered through booksellers or by contacting:

WestBow Press
A Division of Thomas Nelson & Zondervan
1663 Liberty Drive
Bloomington, IN 47403
www.westbowpress.com
844-714-3454

Scripture quotations are from the ESV Bible® (The Holy Bible, English Standard Version®), copyright © 2001 by Crossway Bibles, a publishing ministry of Good News Publishers. Used by permission. All rights reserved.

ISBN: 978-1-6642-8256-8 (sc)
ISBN: 978-1-6642-8257-5 (hc)
ISBN: 978-1-6642-8255-1 (e)

Library of Congress Control Number: 2022920262

Print information available on the last page.

WestBow Press rev. date: 11/17/2022

For we know that if the tent that is our earthly home is destroyed, we have a building from God, a house not made with hands, eternal in the heavens.

2 Corinthians 5:1

CONTENTS

TEN KEY REFERENCES

Blessed be the God and Father of our Lord Jesus Christ, who has blessed us in Christ with every spiritual blessing in the heavenly places, even as he chose us in him before the foundation of the world, that we should be holy and blameless before him. In love he predestined us for adoption to himself as sons through Jesus Christ, according to the purpose of his will, to the praise of his glorious grace, with which he has blessed us in the Beloved. In him we have redemption through his blood, the forgiveness of our trespasses, according to the riches of his grace, which he lavished upon us, in all wisdom and insight making known to us the mystery of his will, according to his purpose, which he set forth in Christ as a plan for the fullness of time, to unite all things in him, things in heaven and things on earth.

In him we have obtained an inheritance, having been predestined according to the purpose of him who works all things according to the counsel of his will, so that we who were the first to hope in Christ might be to the praise of his glory. In him you also, when you heard the word of truth, the gospel of your salvation, and believed in him, were sealed with the promised Holy Spirit, who is the guarantee of our inheritance until we acquire possession of it, to the praise of his glory.

Ephesians 1:3-14

"Let not your hearts be troubled. Believe in God; believe also in me. In my Father's house are many rooms. If it were not so, would I have told you that I go to prepare a place for you? And if I go and prepare a place for you, I will come again and will take you to myself, that where I am you may be also. And you know the way to where I am going." Thomas said to him, "Lord, we do not know where you are going. How can we know the way?" Jesus said to him, "I am the way, and the truth, and the life. No one comes to the Father except through me. If you had known me, you would have known my Father also. From now on you do know him and have seen him."

John 14:1-7

Jesus said to her, "I am the resurrection and the life. Whoever believes in me, though he die, yet shall he live,

John 11:25

For we know that if the tent that is our earthly home is destroyed, we have a building from God, a house not made with hands, eternal in the heavens. For in this tent we groan, longing to put on our heavenly dwelling, if indeed by putting it on we may not be found naked. For while we are still in this tent, we groan, being burdened—not that we would be unclothed, but that we would be further clothed, so that what is mortal may be swallowed up by life. He who has prepared us for this very thing is God, who has given us the Spirit as a guarantee.

So we are always of good courage. We know that while we are at home in the body we are away from the Lord, for we walk by faith, not by sight. Yes, we are of good courage, and we would rather be away from the body and at home with the Lord. So whether we are at home or away, we make it our aim to please him. For we must all appear before the judgment seat of Christ, so that each one may receive what is due for what he has done in the body, whether good or evil.

2 Corinthians 5:1-10

For I consider that the sufferings of this present time are not worth comparing with the glory that is to be revealed to us. For the creation waits with eager longing for the revealing of the sons of God. For the creation was subjected to futility, not willingly, but because of him who subjected it, in hope that the creation itself will be set free from its bondage to corruption and obtain the freedom of the glory of the children of God.

For we know that the whole creation has been groaning together in the pains of childbirth until now. And not only the creation, but we ourselves, who have the firstfruits of the Spirit, groan inwardly as we wait eagerly for adoption as sons, the redemption of our bodies. For in this hope we were saved. Now hope that is seen is not hope. For who hopes for what he sees? But if we hope for what we do not see, we wait for it with patience.

Romans 8:18-25

So we do not lose heart. Though our outer self is wasting away, our inner self is being renewed day by day. For this light momentary affliction is preparing for us an eternal weight of glory beyond all comparison, as we look not to the things that are seen but to the things that are unseen. For the things that are seen are transient, but the things that are unseen are eternal.

2 Corinthians 4:16-18

If the Spirit of him who raised Jesus from the dead dwells in you, he who raised Christ Jesus from the dead will also give life to your mortal bodies through his Spirit who dwells in you.

Romans 8:11

For you have died, and your life is hidden with Christ in God. When Christ who is your life appears, then you also will appear with him in glory.

Colossians 3:3-4

But he [Steven], full of the Holy Spirit, gazed into heaven and saw the glory of God, and Jesus standing at the right hand of God. And he said, "Behold, I see the heavens opened, and the Son of Man standing at the right hand of God."

Acts 7:55-56

But our citizenship is in heaven, and from it we await a Savior, the Lord Jesus Christ, who will transform our lowly body to be like his glorious body, by the power that enables him even to subject all things to himself.

Therefore, my brothers, whom I love and long for, my joy and crown, stand firm thus in the Lord, my beloved.

Philippians 3:20 - 4:1

These ten scripture references assembled above are the basis for this bible study lesson of life to life in Christ.

For our salvation is for God, of God, by God, in God, through God, because of God, and for the glory of God, lest any man would boast. And to seek and understand that our life is not our own.

These verses are just a start, for as you read, I pray that you will see that life in and through Jesus is the epitome of who we are. That at death, true life begins for all who believe in Jesus.

Father, glorify yourself and your Son as we study your word, and may you change our hearts to see you in all splendor and glory. In Jesus's name, I ask, Amen.

DEDICATIONS

To my Lord and Savior, Jesus Christ. He revealed Himself to me when I was 14 years old and enabled me to believe that He died for me and to show the sin within me and my need for Him.

To my wife, Sandy. Who is now with Jesus after suffering an unexpected fatal heart attack on November 29, 2021.

To my son Chris, my daughter Ashley, her husband Nick, and their daughters Hailey, Aubrey, Savannah, and Olivia. To offer you comfort through God's word that we will see mom again. And there is hope for us to the day God calls each of us home.

And to the reader of this book. For you to know that faith in Christ brings us eternal life realized at our last breath.

I pray that as I study and search the Word of God, I find and then share my heart of this study with those who are like-minded in wondering about life-to-life for those who believe.

Jesus doesn't speak of dying, but of sleeping for those who believe in Him. But, as we will learn, this body we now occupy is corrupted by sin. But the Holy Spirit within us is our surety towards our Heavenly bodies. And our spiritual bodies will one day be joined with our new resurrected immortal bodies when Christ returns.

So be of good cheer, for this world is not our home, for we are just passing through!

APPRECIATION

First and foremost, I want to thank my Lord and Savior, Jesus Christ. For everything, For life, physical and eternal. For a life lived. Here and now, and one day before You in glory. All things are for you, Lord, and I praise you for revealing Yourself and enabling me to see You and to believe! All glory and honor are Yours!

After my salvation, I thank you, Jesus, for giving me Sandy as my wife for a season of life on this Earth. And to our children, she bore, and for the next generation of grandchildren. Our prayer Father, Lord Jesus, is that you will continue to glorify yourself within the family legacy you have started in us, and that You will save each generation from Sandy and me, trusting that this is within your will.

And again, Lord, to the people you have placed before me as I write about You, my Lord, Savior, and my life! I appreciate the friendships and the common bond of Christ with my proofreaders.

To Don Lind. Who has journeyed with me in each book I have written. I am using a few business terms as you have been my trusted advisor. My sounding board to the proof of concepts. My friend. Thank you, Don, for your support. For being there as I write. For being there when a trial hits me, and for your advice. Also, for having a good ear for listening. Thank you!

To Tom Kreider. The bond with Tom has many links, dating back to the season of our church time at Bible Baptist. Tom's wife, Meladee, and another lady at church, Marsha Ellis, became close friends through our family's church relationships.

Sandy, Meladee, and Marsha. As you also know, Tom, our wives, grew close during this time. But you probably didn't know that I called them The Three Musketeers when Sandy would tell me about their shopping adventures.

So within the providence of God, the other fiber that connects Tom and me is that Tom's wife, Meladee, preceded Sandy's passing by about 2-3 years. And in Sandy's death, God has brought you and me together, for each of us to bear one another's burdens and sorrow. So thank you, Tom, for our enduring friendship, now strengthened further in God's grace through the loss of our wives, and I appreciate your insights and feedback on the experiences and emotions we have in common.

To my sister Barb. God called mom home in 2017. Then, two years later, dad also went home. Now, in mid-2021, God has called home our last surviving uncle. And in November, He also brought Sandy home. And as I wrap up this book, our last surviving aunt went home to be with the Lord in May. These last six years have witnessed God's love within our family of the grace through faith He has blessed our family with - now being made complete as He called our loved ones home. So, Sis, you and I have moved up to the pole position. [Add your favorite smiley emoji here.]

Although we have been miles apart, I appreciate your taking the time to help review my writings. I hope this study has been as joyous for you as it has been for me.

To my mother-in-law, Nola. It's been hard losing a wife for me, but losing a daughter is equally difficult for you, mom. Life order assumes that the young will grow old, and then when we are 'old,' we will go home to Heaven. There is a unique hurt when a child dies before a parent, and I felt your pain when Sandy died, but I praise God for you and your strength in recovering. Sandy loved you, as you know. And she would do anything and everything she could because of her love for you. Life is not a box of chocolates; for we know that the reward with Christ is much better. (But Sandy and you do like your chocolates.)

As you have read the manuscripts for my first two books, your support for this book holds more value. I praise God for how close we have become, seeing a relationship of mother-in-law as another mom to me stepping in. Thank you, mom, for being Sandy's mother and my mother-in-law and for our prayer times and bible studies together. I chuckle every night after our prayer time that you say, "If the Good Lord is willing, I'll talk to you tomorrow, or if not you, then to Sandy," and for the reader, at the time of this writing, I wrote this when mom recently turned 89.

And to a Few of Sandy's Lifetime of Friendships

Next, it is of value to my family to mention our mom's friendships over the years. In life, we all have a journey and path to travel, and the following folks came into an intersection with mom and me as we did life together with other people. As you continue the journey of life that God has given you, maybe remembering Mom's path and how God used her to touch others can help us not forget her and be better aware of God's role in our lives. To love God and to love people.

To start, I want to thank the sales team at the local neighborhood furniture store, where Sandy was employed before she died. To Jerry Palmer, the Store Manager. To Portia Evans, the Sales Manager. And to the staff of Danielle Beighley, Megan Moran, Kayla Payne, Bill Ruether, Janeth Stang, and Lori Stillwagon. What a blessing you were and are to Sandy and me.

You became a family to us as you integrated Sandy's return into the workforce in 2018 after being a stay-at-home wife and mom for 30 years. Sandy would come home from work every night and share her day with me. And to hear about her client's needs, both in furniture and life, how she enjoyed working with you, and the company she loved to represent. Each night she would tell me all the stories and antics of living life together each day within the store - it was a joy for me to experience secondhand as well. Thank you for taking the job and turning it into a blessing for us both.

And also, know that you all were in our prayers each night. And know that through and in Jesus, we will one day see her again.

And to Sandy's auction friends, Joan Voegtly and Linda Stoffel. Oh, the laughter you shared - and the dry humor. Sandy loved your craziness and the times you shared.

And to her crafting group. She loved you ladies and the times of crafting together, even when you met in our garage. What a sight you all were in your Covid masks as you met at our home during Covid-19. As if nothing was different at all! She so enjoyed you, crafting, and the times together.

And to her special individual friendships. To Sandy, she viewed all of her friends as best friends, for she had the gift of making friends from acquaintances.

To lifelong friend Leslie Quinn, who was Sandy's bridesmaid. Oh, how Sandy loved you, Leslie. You two have the longest legacy as active friends, and even after Sandy's passing, you honored that friendship by bringing a few meals to support the family and me. Thank you.

To friendships from our church relationships, Beth Leapline and Lyda Word, adding to already mentioned Joan, Linda, Meladee, and Marsha.

And to the various church groups over the years and the bible study groups, we were members. To the youth groups we hosted at our homes. To all the years of participating in the Easter Cantatas. And to the baby nurseries and kitchen duties, she supported. Sandy enjoyed serving.

To former neighborhood friends of many years ago, Patty Shock and Marsha Nuzzo

Patty, when you and Sandy were on the phone after you moved westward, I could count on it being for hours, knowing how much you supported each other. Although being long-distance apart, it was like you were in the same room, the enduring friendship of time and distance.

And Marsha. You and Sandy quickly bonded when our daughters were in kindergarten together. Oh, the life as families we shared through our girls. First from school. As a neighbor and then through the church, Sandy so enjoyed your friendship and the bond you also had in crafting.

And even the friendships Sandy and I made eating at restaurants, especially meeting and befriending Pam and Jim at the Olive Garden.

I am sure I am missing many others, but to my family, know that Mom/Grammy loved making friends, and friendships were important to her as to who she is. Jesus tells us that the world will see that we are His disciples if we love God and people.

I can only imagine the friendships she now has in Heaven, as I hope to share later in this book about life in Heaven.

My Purpose in Writing

Where do I begin? When I retired from my sales career in October of 2018, I sensed that now in my early sixties, my health was showing more signs of age. And I thought, well, I better get my house in order, per the chance that God would call me home sooner than later.

So I began documenting the finances, the passwords, and the locations of the essential papers so that my wife would have an easier time finding our 'stuff,' should God call me home first.

And within my plan, I began writing, at first, to my family a book on how Jesus saved me from my sins. And to also declare how God has all things under His control. And I wanted to leave them a legacy of my faith in Christ to encourage, instruct, and love them. And in this, it is the most important thing I could leave to them when God calls me home.

After writing the first book, 'The Sovereignty of God in Our Daily Lives,' I started to sense a call to continue writing. So the second book came relatively quickly, picking up from where the first book left off. This book is entitled 'En Route to the Mount of Olives – Matthew 24' and is about the disciples' two questions of Jesus right before the Passover - Palm Sunday: what is the sign of your return, and what is the sign of the end of the age?

As I sent that book to the publisher in early November 2021, God called my beloved wife home a few weeks later. Her sudden passing shocked our family, for my wife had no symptoms or warning signs of heart disease.

So before she died, I was thinking about authoring other books on biblical studies. One area I was studying was in regards to the Holy Spirit. Another subject I felt called to examine was our sinfulness. And then the last book on my radar is the book you now hold in your hands - At Heaven's Door. At Heaven's Door was the last book I was planning to write for when I had some inkling that my time was nearing. That in this book, it would be my last love letter to my family.

BUT NOW, with my wife's passing from life to life, I am drawn to writing about Heaven, seeing that she is now face-to-face with Jesus!

This book is partly my grieving therapy – in my missing her smile, laughter, her voice in talking together, and loving touch. But it is also my joy to search the scriptures to see what Jesus says about Heaven. And by seeking to understand more about life in Heaven and being with Jesus, Sandy is now living and enjoying.

So whether you also miss a loved one who is now home with the Lord or you sense God will call you to come home soon, I present this book in love and comfort to know life does not end in death for those in Christ. For our citizenship is not of this world, but in Heaven. And the Glory of Jesus is the pearl of great price! And with that last breath, our faith becomes realized. So I pray that God will grant us both - His grace and wisdom through His Spirit as we study this subject together.

Blessed be the God and Father of our Lord Jesus Christ, the Father of mercies and God of all comfort, who comforts us in all our affliction, so that we may be able to comfort those who are in any affliction, with the comfort with which we ourselves are comforted by God. For as we share abundantly in Christ's sufferings, so through Christ we share abundantly in comfort too.

(2 Corinthians 1:3-5)

INTRODUCTION

As I previously stated, this book fulfills the trilogy of the three books I felt moved to write - towards my family, my friends, and the reader.

As you review the Table of Contents, you will see many of those questions I raised to myself [and even to God, Jesus, and the Holy Spirit] as I began searching with the focus within the Bible for wisdom and understanding.

Some of the questions I found have clear answers within the Bible. With the other queries I raised, I can draw realistic conclusions. And yet a few other questions I have posed still beg for validation.

And lastly, before we start our studies - and as my career in sales has taught me, and with Biblical support as a pattern to follow, repetition helps convey the points for the clarity of the intended message. Sometimes reiteration is used for emphasis. Other times I use it to make a strong point. But at all times, to help the reader capture the intent of the message sent is the message received as intended by me, the writer.

As I have offered in my previous books, I present a section of pertinent scriptures aligned with the subjects for the rest of the book. Then I will use these verses to write about the topics by chapter. And as I write, I will often present the Bible study with the knowledge that my wife, Sandy, is now in the presence of Jesus. So to ask and then address the questions I ask through the Bible verses I uncover through the filter of my wife, who now is in Heaven.

So now to a bit of family background to set the stage, tone, and study. Next, an open letter for my grandchildren, for the love of Grammy and me, is deep and genuine.

SANDY, MOM ... GRAMMY

Grieving the loss of a loved one is hard to explain to someone who hasn't experienced it firsthand, but to those who have, you know the pain of missing a beloved.

My children know my story about Mom and me. Still, for my grandkids and possibly their kids, if God provides in the future, I want to share with my grandchildren how God brought Grammy and me together and how Jesus was our focus in life and throughout our marriage.

To my Grandchildren, How Grammy and I Met.

So Grammy [Sandy, for those following along] and I first met working in a local steel mill in 1981. At that time, I was working during the years after the 1973 oil embargo that affected the gasoline supply chain throughout the world.

I followed my father into the mill after leaving college in May of 1977. The company hired me as a steelworker in January of 1978. What a life-changing experience. I went from an academic environment into a dark, dirty, dangerous steel mill environment.

From the start, I began a four-year stint of working swing shifts, seven days a week, which spanned from the first days of my starting work into the early part of 1982.

As a young man of 21, it was hard work, but the pay was good, the job was dangerous, and my life was routine and predictably the same every day. I woke up, packed my lunch, went to work, came home, and ate dinner, or breakfast, whichever shift I was finishing. Then I went to sleep. Repeat.

A steel mill from the 1970s is the same steel mill of the 1940s and 50s. The lighting is poor. The dirt and steel dust are inches thick and are everywhere. In the winter, the mill is freezing, and in the summer, it's an oven. Banging pipes, running machines, and cranes overhead moving "iron" make for a noisy and dangerous environment. You had to be on your toes every second you were in the plant, for there is no such thing as a minor accident in a mill.

Fast forward to August 1981. I trained as a machinist on the big B & O Cut-Off machines soon after my hire. This mill produced drilling pipes of all diameters, including huge 14 3/8" outside diameter, used as drilling casings. And most steel pipes coming out of the piercing mill and through the cooling table and straightener were about 44 feet long.

My job was to manipulate the steel pipe into my cut-off machine after it had passed the inspection table, transported by giant electric run rolls along the center wall of the mill. Then, it would kick onto the cut-off table, my work area. My coworker would bring the long pipe into his machine on the front side of this big table, and lock it into his cut-off machine. Then the cut-off machine would turn the 44foot long steel pipe as he operated the cut-off machine and cut the raw, jagged end of the steel pipe into a smooth, chamfered, semi-finished end. Then he would send it away from his machine, kicking it out on the 65-foot holding table between us. It would then roll down to my machine to follow the same process, and I would cut off the back end.

So being on the production line, we ran our table during our shift, striving to beat the production speed of the steel pipe being made and sent to us.

When I finished each pipe, I would send it back out of my machine, and kick it onto the inspection table, dropping it into the 'hookup' bay after inspection. Then an overhead crane would come by to take a bale of our cleaned-edged pipe down to the threading department to finish processing.

Having done this for about three years, God gave me the skills to be quite good at the role. It was a hard job. Dangerous to run this machine and move heavy ends of steel pipe that would fall to the floor of the crop bucket as I finished cutting the end of the pipe - as those hot filings would fly off the machine as the carbide tools would cut the steel pipe as it spun.

So one day in August of 1981, as I was operating my machine, I was talking with God (as I do most times during my day.) But today, I told Him my heart was lonely, for I felt a hole within me. I so wanted to be married and have a family of my own. I always admired my grandfather and grandmother, for they were married for over fifty years, and I witnessed their love for each other. So I had a strong desire to follow their pattern, but I did not see how it would be possible to work every day without a break. So, I wanted to be like my parents and grandparents, having love in the house and having love endure. So I asked God how I would meet a good Christian woman working seven days a week in a steel mill, no less.

God Works in Unexpected Ways.

In His mercy and grace, God answered my prayer a month later.

In a late effort not to 'burn-out' their workers, the company decided to add a fourth production shift inside the plant, rotating four crews - versus the current three daily shift changes. Working with the fourth crew gave everyone two days off a week, which gave the workers time to regroup.

It was about the second week of September 1981, and a group of new hires came through the mill. As this group of about fifteen people walked along the safety path, they stopped by my work area, about 30 feet from my machine. And the guard giving the plant tour gave an overview to the group of what happens at my work area.

I remember this as if it were yesterday. Behind the walkway was a heat-treating furnace that tempered the steel pipe to make the steel 'hardened.' There was a bank of soot-tinted windows behind the cooling table, with a broken window to the right. It was a sunny morning, and the sun came through the broken window opening, offering the only bright light within the dark plant floor. And as I was watching the new hires take the tour, Grammy was standing there with the others. The light through the broken window fell behind Grammy, casting its light around her like a halo! She was listening to the guard with the other new hires. And my jaw dropped. I saw her for the first time and knew God had sent her to me. I didn't know her name or where she lived. Or even how old or if she were single. On this day, Grammy was the brightest sight in a chilly dark mill, and I knew God had sent her for me. Indeed, it was love at first sight.

I shut off my machine, and as they left to go down to the threading floor, I went to the safety aisle and watched as they walked away. And I remembered thanking God for sending Grammy to the mill right then and there.

Long story short, she was assigned to work the same shift as me in the following weeks. And she was also given to work as a laborer at my cut-off machine. I quickly found out that she was indeed a Christian. In addition, she was single - a year younger than me - and she also had a mutual interest in talking.

God is sovereign, Amen? Amen!

On October 20, 1981, we went on our first date. And on January 29, 1982, we were married! Praise God! And had Grammy lived only two more months, we would have been married forty years on January 29, 2022. Thank you, Lord, for giving us the time we had together!

After Grammy and I were married, the bottom soon fell out of the oil industry, and intense exploration for new wells collapsed in 1982. Grammy was laid-off from the mill a few months after we married, never returning to the mill. Translation. God brought Grammy and me together through her short time in the mill and then took us away from the mill, starting first with Grammy. Then, two and a half years later, the mill closed its doors, to which I never returned. The best part of my mill experience was the wedding of Grammy. The best part of the oil collapse was me leaving the mill to where God called Grammy and me next. We went in uncertainty – but knew God had a better plan for us.

And now, with your uncle Chris being born in 1984, and then your mom 18 months later, God sends me back to college under a trade readjustment program of the time right before your mom was born. What a blessing on many fronts. Although Grammy and I were without steady work for the next few years, God always provided for us. As a result, we never missed rent or bill payments and always had food on the table.

There are many more details about how God worked in Grammy's and my life, but for this writing, I want you to know, see and understand that God is sovereign in everything. And that He is our Provider. And that He covets our love, prayers, adoration, and worship.

The Call.

So, kids, now that Grammy is with Jesus, I want you to know how much you are loved. By Jesus, by Grammy, and by me. And that speaks well to the reader following along, too. As Christians, Christ's love is pouring into each of us, and you, too, are so loved! So as we journey together in this study - ask. Ask God for wisdom and understanding. And ask God for His grace and mercy to be upon you. For His namesake and your benefit.

And Finish. Finish Strong; Finish Well!

Therefore, since we are surrounded by so great a cloud of witnesses, let us also lay aside every weight and sin which clings so closely, and let us run with endurance the race that is set before us, looking to Jesus, the founder and perfecter of our faith, who for the joy that was set before him endured the cross, despising the shame, and is seated at the right hand of the throne of God.

(Hebrews 12:1-2)

"Cloud of witnesses?" Stay tuned; more to be said about this later.

FIELD OF SCRIPTURES

As with my previous books, I feel it extremely important to position the groupings of scripture as a separate section I have in mind for the books I write. My heart is to share that God's words are more important than mine. And if folks would focus on just sitting down, reading, and studying the scripture verses that follow - through prayer and with the guidance of the Holy Spirit- it would fulfill my goal for this book.

In my studies, more verses speak of life-to-life in Heaven, the Kingdom of God, the New Heaven, Earth, and Jerusalem, and the progression of time in Christ than one would imagine.

As I started compiling the verses as a basis for this study, my heart filled with joy in God, giving me a more extensive glimpse of what is in store for us who believe. And I pray that you, too, will be blessed in seeing His Glory as to what lies ahead!

The Path of Life.

> You make known to me the path of life; in your presence there is fullness of joy; at your right hand are pleasures forevermore. (Psalms 16:11; emphasis added)

> For the LORD is righteous; he loves righteous deeds; the upright shall behold his face. (Psalms 11:7)

> As for me, I shall behold your face in righteousness; when I awake, I shall be satisfied with your likeness. (Psalms 17:15)

One thing have I asked of the LORD, that will I seek after: that I may dwell in the house of the LORD all the days of my life, to gaze upon the beauty of the LORD and to inquire in his temple. (Psalms 27:4)

Whom have I in heaven but you? And there is nothing on earth that I desire besides you. My flesh and my heart may fail, but God is the strength of my heart and my portion forever. (Psalms 73:25-26)

If then you have been raised with Christ, seek the things that are above, where Christ is, seated at the right hand of God. Set your minds on things that are above, not on things that are on earth. For you have died, and your life is hidden with Christ in God. When Christ who is your life appears, then you also will appear with him in glory. (Colossians 3:1-4)

"The secret things belong to the Lord our God, but the things that are revealed belong to us and to our children forever, that we may do all the words of this law. (Deuteronomy 29:29)

Born of the Spirit. (Born Again)

I will sprinkle clean water on you, and you shall be clean from all your uncleannesses, and from all your idols I will cleanse you. And I will give you a new heart, and a new spirit I will put within you. And I will remove the heart of stone from your flesh and give you a heart of flesh. And **I will put my Spirit within you**, and cause you to walk in my statutes and be careful to obey my rules. (Ezekiel 36:25-27; emphasis added)

And even if our gospel is veiled, it is veiled to those who are perishing. In their case the god of this world has blinded the minds of the unbelievers, to keep them from seeing the light of the gospel of the glory of Christ, who is the image of God. For what we proclaim is not ourselves, but Jesus Christ as Lord, with ourselves as your servants for Jesus' sake. **For God, who said, "Let light shine out of darkness," has shone in our hearts to give the light of the knowledge of the glory of God in the face of Jesus Christ.** (2 Corinthians 4:3-6; emphasis added)

For the wages of sin is death, but the free gift of God is eternal life in Christ Jesus our Lord. (Romans 6:23)

But what does it say? "The word is near you, in your mouth and in your heart" (that is, the word of faith that we proclaim); because, if you confess with your mouth that Jesus is Lord and believe in your heart that God raised him from the dead, you will be saved. For with the heart one believes and is justified, and with the mouth one confesses and is saved. For the Scripture says, "Everyone who believes in him will not be put to shame." For there is no distinction between Jew and Greek; for the same Lord is Lord of all, bestowing his riches on all who call on him. For "everyone who calls on the name of the Lord will be saved." (Romans 10:8-13)

But to all who did receive him, who believed in his name, he gave the right to become children of God, **who were born, not of blood nor of the will of the flesh nor of the will of man, but of God**. (John 1:12-13; emphasis added)

So we are always of good courage. We know that while we are at home in the body we are away from the Lord, for we walk by faith, not by sight. Yes, **we are of good courage,** and we would rather be away from the body and at home with the Lord. (2 Corinthians. 5:4-8; emphasis added)

Blessed be the God and Father of our Lord Jesus Christ, who has blessed us in Christ with every spiritual **blessing in the heavenly places,** (Ephesians 1:3; emphasis added)

For God has not destined us for wrath, but to obtain salvation through our Lord Jesus Christ, who died for us **so that whether we are awake or asleep we might live with him.** (1 Thessalonians 5:9-10; emphasis added)

"Truly, truly, I say to you, **unless one is born of water and the Spirit, he cannot enter the kingdom of God.** That which is born of the flesh is flesh, and that which is born of the Spirit is spirit. Do not marvel that I said to you, '**You must be born again.**' (John 3:5-7; emphasis added)

"**We are his workmanship, created in Christ Jesus for good works, which God prepared beforehand, that we should walk in them.** (Ephesians 2:10; emphasis added)

And I will ask the Father, and he will give you another **Helper, to be with you forever,** even **the Spirit of truth, whom the world cannot receive, because it neither sees him nor knows him. You know him, for he dwells with you and will be in you.** (John 14:16-17; emphasis added)

Therefore, **if anyone is in Christ, he is a new creation.** The old has passed away; behold, the new has come. **All this is from God, who through Christ reconciled us to himself.** (2 Corinthians 5:17-18a; emphasis added)

Blessed be the God and Father of our Lord Jesus Christ! According to his great mercy, **he has caused us to be born again to a living hope through the resurrection** of Jesus Christ from the dead, to an inheritance that is **imperishable, undefiled, and unfading, kept in heaven for you,** who by God's power are being guarded through faith for a salvation ready to be revealed in the last time. (1 Peter 1:3-5; emphasis added)

Or do you not know that **your body is a temple of the Holy Spirit within you,** whom you have from God? You are not your own, for **you were bought with a price. So glorify God in your body.** (1 Corinthians 6:17, 19-20; emphasis added)

But when Christ appeared as a high priest of the good things that have come, **then through the greater and more perfect tent (not made with hands, that is, not of this creation)** he entered once for all into the holy places, not by means of the blood of goats and calves but by means of his own blood, thus securing an eternal redemption. For if the blood of goats and bulls, and the sprinkling of defiled persons with the ashes of a heifer, sanctify for the purification of the flesh, how much more will the blood of Christ, who through the eternal Spirit offered himself without blemish to God, purify our conscience from dead works to serve the living God.

Therefore he is the mediator of a new covenant, so that those who are called may receive the promised eternal inheritance, since a death has occurred that redeems them from the transgressions committed under the first covenant. (Hebrews 9:11-15; emphasis added)

These things God has revealed to us through the Spirit. For the Spirit searches everything, even the depths of God. For who knows a person's thoughts except the spirit of that person, which is in him? So also no one comprehends the thoughts of God except the Spirit of God. Now we have received not the spirit of the world, but the Spirit who is from God, that we might understand the things freely given us by God. And we impart this in words not taught by human wisdom but taught by the Spirit, interpreting spiritual truths to those who are spiritual.

And I will ask the Father, and **he will give you another Helper, to be with you forever, even the Spirit of truth, whom the world cannot receive, because it neither sees him nor knows him. You know him, for he dwells with you and will be in you.** (John 14:16-17; emphasis added)

The natural person does not accept the things of the Spirit of God, for they are folly to him, and he is not able to understand them because they are spiritually discerned. The spiritual person judges all things, but is himself to be judged by no one. "For who has understood the mind of the Lord so as to instruct him?" **But we have the mind of Christ.** (1 Corinthians 2:10-16; emphasis added)

You, however, are not in the flesh but in the Spirit, if in fact the Spirit of God dwells in you. Anyone who does not have the Spirit of Christ does not belong to him. But if Christ is in you, although the body is dead because of sin, the Spirit is life because of righteousness. **If the Spirit of him who raised Jesus from the dead dwells in you, he who raised Christ Jesus from the dead will also give life to your mortal bodies through his Spirit who dwells in you.** (Romans 8:9-11; emphasis added)

Blessed be the God and Father of our Lord Jesus Christ, **who has blessed us in Christ with every spiritual blessing in the heavenly places,** even as **he chose us in him before the foundation of the world,** that we should be holy and blameless before him. In love he predestined us for adoption to himself as sons through Jesus Christ, **according to the purpose of his will, to the praise of his glorious grace,** with which he has blessed us in the Beloved. In him we have redemption through his blood, the forgiveness of our trespasses, according to the riches of his grace, which he lavished upon us, in all wisdom and insight making known to us the mystery of his will, according to his purpose, **which he set forth in Christ as a plan for the fullness of time, to unite all things in him, things in heaven and things on earth.**

In him we have obtained an inheritance, having been predestined according to the purpose of him who works all things according to the counsel of his will, so that **we who were the first to hope in Christ** might be to the praise of his glory. In him you also, when you heard the word of truth, the gospel of your salvation, and believed in him, *were sealed with the promised Holy Spirit, who is the guarantee of our inheritance until we acquire possession of it, to the praise of his glory.*

(Ephesians 1:3-14; emphasis added)

The Days of Life on Earth.

Your eyes saw my unformed substance; in your book were written, every one of them, the days that were formed for me, when as yet there was none of them. (Psalms 139:16)

Since his [man's] days are determined, and the number of his months is with you, and you have appointed his limits that he cannot pass. (Job 14:5)

No man has power to retain the spirit, or power over the day of death. (Ecclesiastes 8:8a)

A good name is better than precious ointment, and the day of death than the day of birth. (Ecclesiastes 7:1)

So we are always of good courage. We know that while we are at home in the body we are away from the Lord, for we walk by faith, not by sight. Yes, we are of good courage, and we would rather be away from the body and at home with the Lord. (2 Corinthians 5:6-8)

Moreover, it is required of stewards that they be found faithful. (1 Corinthians 4:2)

Our Tent, Citizenship, The Resurrection.

Tent – Our Mortal Bodies.

For **we know that if the tent that is our earthly home is destroyed, we have a building from God, a house not made with hands, eternal in the heavens.** For in this tent we groan, longing to put on our heavenly dwelling, if indeed by putting it on we may not be found naked.

For while we are still in this tent, we groan, being burdened—not that we would be unclothed, but that we would be further clothed, so that what is mortal may be swallowed up by life. He who has prepared us for this very thing is God, **who has given us the Spirit as a guarantee.**

So we are always of good courage. We know that **while we are at home in the body we are away from the Lord, for we walk by faith,** not by sight. Yes, we are of good courage, and **we would rather be away from the body** and at home with the Lord. <u>So whether we are at home or</u> <u>away, we make it our aim to please him.</u> For we must all appear before the judgment seat of Christ, so that each one may receive what is due for what he has done in the body, whether good or evil. (2 Corinthians 5:1-10; emphasis added)

Citizenship is in Heaven.

But our citizenship is in heaven, and from it we await a Savior, the Lord Jesus Christ, who will transform our lowly body to be like his glorious body, by the power that enables him even to subject all things to himself. (Philippians 3:20-21)

So then you are no longer strangers and aliens, but you are **fellow citizens with the saints and members of the household of God,** built on the foundation of the apostles and prophets, Christ Jesus himself being the cornerstone, in whom **the whole structure, being joined together, grows into a holy temple in the Lord In him** you also are being built together into a dwelling place for God by the Spirit. (Ephesians 2:19-22; emphasis added)

One thing have I asked of the LORD, that will I seek after: that I may dwell in the house of the LORD all the days of my life, to gaze upon the beauty of the LORD and to inquire in his temple. (Psalms 27:4)

If then you have been raised with Christ, seek the things that are above, where Christ is, seated at the right hand of God. Set your minds on things that are above, not on things that are on earth. For you have died, and your life is hidden with Christ in God. When Christ who is your life appears, then you also will appear with him in glory. (Colossians 3:1-4)

Spiritual Bodies.

It is sown a natural body; it is raised a spiritual body. If there is a natural body, there is also a spiritual body. (1 Corinthians 15:44)

For we know that if the tent that is our earthly home is destroyed, **we have a building from God, a house not made with hands**, eternal in the heavens. For in this tent we groan, **longing to put on our heavenly dwelling**, if indeed by putting it on we may not be found naked. (2 Corinthians 5:1-3; emphasis added)

As you come to him, a living stone rejected by men but in the sight of God chosen and precious, **you yourselves like living stones are being built up as a spiritual house**, to be a holy priesthood, to offer spiritual sacrifices acceptable to God through Jesus Christ. (1 Peter 2:4-5; emphasis added)

Do you not know that you are God's temple and that **God's Spirit dwells in you?** (1 Corinthians 3:16; emphasis added)

By the Holy Spirit who dwells within us, guard the good deposit entrusted to you. (2 Timothy 1:14)

You, however, are not in the flesh but in the Spirit, if in fact the Spirit of God dwells in you. Anyone who does not have the Spirit of Christ does not belong to him. But if Christ is in you, although the body is dead because of sin, the Spirit is life because of righteousness. If the Spirit of him who raised Jesus from the dead dwells in you, he who raised Christ Jesus from the dead will also give life to your mortal bodies through his Spirit who dwells in you. (Romans 8:9-11)

For while we are still in this tent, we groan, being burdened—not that we would be unclothed, but that we would be further clothed, **so that what is mortal may be swallowed up by life.** He who has prepared us for this very thing is God, who has given us the Spirit as a guarantee. (2 Corinthians 5:4-5; emphasis added)

Resurrection.

So is it with the resurrection of the dead. What is sown is perishable; what is raised is imperishable. It is sown in dishonor; it is raised in glory. It is sown in weakness; it is raised in power. (1 Corinthians 15:42-43)

Since we have the same spirit of faith according to what has been written, "I believed, and so I spoke," we also believe, and so we also speak, **knowing that he who raised the Lord Jesus will raise us also with Jesus and bring us with you into his presence.** For it is all for your sake, so that as grace extends to more and more people it may increase thanksgiving, **to the glory of God.**

So we do not lose heart. **Though our outer self is wasting away, our inner self is being renewed day by day. For this light momentary affliction is preparing for us an eternal weight of glory beyond all comparison, as we look not to the things that are seen but to the things that are unseen. For the things that are seen are transient, but the things that are unseen are eternal.** (2 Corinthians 4:13-18; emphasis added)

But we do not want you to be uninformed, brothers, about those who are asleep, that you may not grieve as others do who have no hope. For since we believe that Jesus died and rose again, even so, through Jesus, God will bring with him those who have fallen asleep. For this we declare to you by a word from the Lord, that we who are alive, who are left until the coming of the Lord, will not precede those who have fallen asleep. For the Lord himself will descend from heaven with a cry of command, with the voice of an archangel, and with the sound of the trumpet of God. And the dead in Christ will rise first. Then we who are alive, who are left, will be caught up **together with them in the clouds to meet the Lord in the air, and so we will always be with the Lord.** Therefore encourage one another with these words. (1 Thessalonians 4:13-18; emphasis added)

"Immediately after the tribulation of those days the sun will be darkened, and the moon will not give its light, and the stars will fall from heaven, and the powers of the heavens will be shaken. Then will appear in heaven the sign of the Son of Man, and then all the tribes of the earth will mourn, and they will see the Son of Man coming on the clouds of heaven with power and great glory. And he will send out his angels with a loud trumpet call, and they will gather his elect from the four winds, from one end of heaven to the other. (Matthew 24:29-31)

The Tent of God.

But when Christ appeared as a high priest of the good things that have come, then through **the greater and more perfect tent** (not made with hands, that is, not of this creation) **he entered once for all into the holy places,** not by means of the blood of goats and calves but by means of his own blood, thus securing an eternal redemption. (Hebrews 9:11-12; emphasis added)

It was now about the sixth hour, and there was darkness over the whole land until the ninth hour, while the sun's light failed. **And the curtain of the temple was torn in two.** Then Jesus, calling out with a loud voice, said, "Father, into your hands I commit my spirit!" And having said this he breathed his last. Now when the centurion saw what had taken place, he praised God, saying, "Certainly this man was innocent!" (Luke 23:44-47; emphasis added)

Heaven.

In my Father's house are many rooms. If it were not so, would I have told you that I go to prepare a place for you? And if I go and prepare a place for you, I will come again and will take you to myself, that where I am you may be also. (John 14:2-3)

And he said, "Jesus, remember me when you come into your kingdom." And he said to him, "Truly, I say to you, today you will be with me in paradise." (Luke 23:42-43)

Have this mind among yourselves, which is yours in Christ Jesus, who, though he was in the form of God, did not count equality with God a thing to be grasped, but emptied himself, by taking the form of a servant, being born in the likeness of men. And being found in human form, he humbled himself by becoming obedient to the point of death, even death on a cross. (Philippians 2:5-8)

"Enter by the narrow gate. For the gate is wide and the way is easy that leads to destruction, and those who enter by it are many. For the gate is narrow and the way is hard that leads to life, and those who find it are few. (Matthew 7:13-14)

Visions into Heaven.

By Steven.

But he [Steven], full of the Holy Spirit, gazed into heaven and saw the glory of God, and Jesus standing at the right hand of God. And he said, "Behold, I see the heavens opened, and the Son of Man standing at the right hand of God." (Acts 7:55-56)

And as they were stoning Stephen, he called out, "Lord Jesus, receive my spirit." And falling to his knees he cried out with a loud voice, "Lord, do not hold this sin against them." And when he had said this, he fell asleep. (Acts 7:59-60)

By John.

At once I was in the Spirit, and behold, a throne stood in heaven, with one seated on the throne. And he who sat there had the appearance of jasper and carnelian, and around the throne was a rainbow that had the appearance of an emerald. Around the throne were twenty-four thrones, and seated on the thrones were twenty-four elders, clothed in white garments, with golden crowns on their heads. From the throne came flashes of lightning, and rumblings and peals of thunder, and before the throne were burning seven torches of fire, which are the seven spirits of God, and before the throne there was as it were a sea of glass, like crystal.

And around the throne, on each side of the throne, are four living creatures, full of eyes in front and behind: the first living creature like a lion, the second living creature like an ox, the third living creature with the face of a man, and the fourth living creature like an eagle in flight. And the four living creatures, each of them with six wings, are full of eyes all around and within, and day and night they never cease to say,

"Holy, holy, holy, is the Lord God Almighty, who was and is and is to come!"

And whenever the living creatures give glory and honor and thanks to him who is seated on the throne, who lives forever and ever, the twenty-four elders fall down before him who is seated on the throne and worship him who lives forever and ever. They cast their crowns before the throne, saying,

"Worthy are you, our Lord and God, to receive glory and honor and power, for you created all things, and by your will they existed and were created." (Revelation 4:2-11)

By Isaiah.

In the year that King Uzziah died I saw the Lord sitting upon a throne, high and lifted up; and the train of his robe filled the temple. Above him stood the seraphim. Each had six wings: with two he covered his face, and with two he covered his feet, and with two he flew. And one called to another and said: "Holy, holy, holy is the LORD of hosts; the whole earth is full of his glory!" And the foundations of the thresholds shook at the voice of him who called, and the house was filled with smoke. (Isaiah 6:1-4)

By Ezekiel.

And from the midst of it came the likeness of four living creatures. And this was their appearance: they had a human likeness, but each had four faces, and each of them had four wings. Their legs were straight, and the soles of their feet were like the sole of a calf's foot. And they sparkled like burnished bronze. Under their wings on their four sides they had human hands. And the four had their faces and their wings thus: their wings touched one another. Each one of them went straight forward, without turning as they went. As for the likeness of their faces, each had a human face. The four had the face of a lion on the right side, the four had the face of an ox on the left side, and the four had the face of an eagle. Such were their faces. And their wings were spread out above. Each creature had two wings, each of which touched the wing of another, while two covered their bodies. And each went straight forward. Wherever the spirit would go, they went, without turning as they went. As for the likeness of the living creatures, their appearance was like burning coals of fire, like the appearance of torches moving to and fro among the living creatures. And the fire was bright, and out of the fire went forth lightning. And the living creatures darted to and fro, like the appearance of a flash of lightning. (Ezekiel 1:5-14)

By Jesus.

"There was a rich man who was clothed in purple and fine linen and who feasted sumptuously every day. And at his gate was laid a poor man named Lazarus, covered with sores, who desired to be fed with what fell from the rich man's table. Moreover, even the dogs came and licked his sores. The poor man died and was carried by the angels to Abraham's side. The rich man also died and was buried, and in Hades, being in torment, he lifted up his eyes and **saw Abraham far off and Lazarus at his side.** And he called out, Father Abraham, have mercy on me, and send Lazarus to dip the end of his finger in water and cool my tongue, for I am in anguish in this flame.' But Abraham said, 'Child, remember that you in your lifetime received your good things, and Lazarus in like manner bad things; but now he is comforted here, and you are in anguish. And besides all this, **between us** and you a great chasm has been fixed, in order that those who would pass from here to you may not be able, and none may cross from there to **us.**' (Luke 16:8-26; emphasis added)

Then the righteous will shine like the sun in the kingdom of their Father. He who has ears, let him hear. (Matthew 13:43)

"**Let not your hearts be troubled. Believe in God; believe also in me. In my Father's house are many rooms.** If it were not so, would I have told you that I go to prepare a place for you? And if I go and prepare a place for you, I will come again and will take you to myself, that where I am you may be also. And you know the way to where I am going." Thomas said to him, "Lord, we do not know where you are going. How can we know the way?" Jesus said to him, "I am the way, and the truth, and the life. No one comes to the Father except through me. If you had known me, you would have known my Father also. From now on you do know him and have seen him." (John 14:1-7; emphasis added)

By Paul.

I know a man in Christ who fourteen years ago was caught up to the third heaven—whether in the body or out of the body I do not know, God knows. And I know that this man was caught up into paradise—whether in the body or out of the body I do not know, God knows— (2 Corinthians 12:2-3)

Yet among the mature we do impart wisdom, although it is not a wisdom of this age or of the rulers of this age, who are doomed to pass away. But we impart a secret and hidden wisdom of God, which God decreed before the ages for our glory. None of the rulers of this age understood this, for if they had, they would not have crucified the Lord of glory. But, as it is written,

"What no eye has seen, nor ear heard, nor the heart of man imagined, what God has prepared for those who love him"— these things God has revealed to us through the Spirit. For the Spirit searches everything, even the depths of God. For who knows a person's thoughts except the spirit of that person, which is in him? So also no one comprehends the thoughts of God except the Spirit of God. Now we have received not the spirit of the world, but the Spirit who is from God, that we might understand the things freely given us by God. And we impart this in words not taught by human wisdom but taught by the Spirit, interpreting spiritual truths to those who are spiritual.

The natural person does not accept the things of the Spirit of God, for they are folly to him, and he is not able to understand them because they are spiritually discerned. The spiritual person judges all things, but is himself to be judged by no one. "For who has understood the mind of the Lord so as to instruct him?" **But we have the mind of Christ**. (1 Corinthians 2:6-16; emphasis added)

For now we see in a mirror dimly, **but then face to face.** Now I know in part; then I shall know fully, even as I have been fully known. (1 Corinthians 13:12; emphasis added)

By the Author of Hebrews.

Therefore from one man, and him as good as dead, were born descendants as many as the stars of heaven and as many as the innumerable grains of sand by the seashore.

These all died in faith, not having received the things promised, but having seen them and greeted them from afar, and having acknowledged that they were strangers and exiles on the earth. For people who speak thus make it clear that they are seeking a homeland. If they had been thinking of that land from which they had gone out, they would have had opportunity to return. **But as it is, they desire a better country, that is, a heavenly one**. Therefore God is not ashamed to be called their God, **for he has prepared for them a city.** (Hebrews 11:12-16; emphasis added)

[Could this be to the time of the New Jerusalem? I explore this in the later part of the book.]

The Inhabitants of Heaven.

God.

Thus says the LORD: "Heaven is my throne, and the earth is my footstool; what is the house that you would build for me, and what is the place of my rest? (Isaiah 66:1)

But I say to you, Do not take an oath at all, either by heaven, for it is the throne of God, or by the earth, for it is his footstool, or by Jerusalem, for it is the city of the great King. (Matthew 5:34-35)

And Jehoshaphat stood in the assembly of Judah and Jerusalem, in the house of the LORD, before the new court, and said, "O LORD, God of our fathers, are you not God in heaven? You rule over all the kingdoms of the nations. In your hand are power and might, so that none is able to withstand you. (2 Chronicles 20:5-6)

The LORD looks down from heaven on the children of man, to see if there are any who understand, who seek after God. (Psalms 14:2)

So then the Lord Jesus, after he had spoken to them, was taken up into heaven and sat down at the right hand of God. (Mark 16:19)

For Christ has entered, not into holy places made with hands, which are copies of the true things, but into heaven itself, now to appear in the presence of God on our behalf. (Hebrews 9:24)

Jesus.

But from now on the Son of Man shall be seated at the right hand of the power of God." (Luke 22:69)

Who is to condemn? Christ Jesus is the one who died—more than that, who was raised—who is at the right hand of God, who indeed is interceding for us. (Romans 8:34)

That he worked in Christ when he raised him from the dead and seated him at his right hand in the heavenly places, far above all rule and authority and power and dominion, and above every name that is named, not only in this age but also in the one to come. And he put all things under his feet and gave him as head over all things to the church, which is his body, the fullness of him who fills all in all. (Ephesians 1:20-23)

Holy Spirit.

It was revealed to them that they were serving not themselves but you, in the things that have now been announced to you through those who preached the good news to you by the Holy Spirit sent from heaven, things into which angels long to look. (1 Peter 1:12)

[Note that the Holy Spirt also lives with the saints who are in Heaven and the Saints who currently alive in this world.]

"If you love me, you will keep my commandments. And I will ask the Father, and he will give you another Helper, to be with you forever, even the Spirit of truth, whom the world cannot receive, because it neither sees him nor knows him. You know him, for he dwells with you and will be in you. (John 14:15-17; emphasis added)

The Seraphim.

Above him stood the seraphim. Each had six wings: with two he covered his face, and with two he covered his feet, and with two he flew. (Isaiah 6:2)

Angels.

The chariots of God are twenty thousand, even thousands of angels. (Psalms 68:17a)

For he shall give his angels charge over thee, to keep thee in all thy ways. (Psalms 91:11)

The Son of man shall send forth his angels, and they shall gather out of his kingdom all things that offend, and them which do iniquity. (Matthew 13:41)

And in the sixth month the angel Gabriel was sent from God unto a city of Galilee, named Nazareth. (Luke 1:26)

Archangels.

[9] But when the archangel Michael, contending with the devil, was disputing about the body of Moses, he did not presume to pronounce a blasphemous judgment, but said, "The Lord rebuke you." (Jude 1:9)

The Four Living Creatures.

And from the midst of it came the likeness of four living creatures. And this was their appearance: they had a human likeness, but each had four faces, and each of them had four wings. Their legs were straight, and the soles of their feet were like the sole of a calf's foot. And they sparkled like burnished bronze. Under their wings on their four sides they had human hands. And the four had their faces and their wings thus: their wings touched one another. Each one of them went straight forward, without turning as they went. As for the likeness of their faces, each had a human face. The four had the face of a lion on the right side, the four had the face of an ox on the left side, and the four had the face of an eagle. Such were their faces. And their wings were spread out above. Each creature had two wings, each of which touched the wing of another, while two covered their bodies. And each went straight forward. Wherever the spirit would go, they went, without turning as they went. As for the likeness of the living creatures, their appearance was like burning coals of fire, like the appearance of torches moving to and fro among the living creatures. And the fire was bright, and out of the fire went forth lightning. And the living creatures darted to and fro, like the appearance of a flash of lightning. (Ezekiel 1:5-14)

And around the throne, on each side of the throne, are four living creatures, full of eyes in front and behind: the first living creature like a lion, the second living creature like an ox, the third living creature with the face of a man, and the fourth living creature like an eagle in flight. And the four living creatures, each of them with six wings, are full of eyes all around and within, and day and night they never cease to say, "Holy, holy, holy, is the Lord God Almighty, who was and is and is to come!" (Revelation 4:6-8)

The Twenty-four Elders.

Around the throne were twenty-four thrones, and seated on the thrones were twenty-four elders, clothed in white garments, with golden crowns on their heads. (Revelation 4:4)

The Saints now in Heaven.

In my Father's house are many rooms. If it were not so, would I have told you that I go to prepare a place for you? (John 14:2)

Satan and his angels.

Now war arose in heaven, Michael and his angels fighting against the dragon. And the dragon and his angels fought back, but he was defeated, and there was no longer any place for them in heaven. (Revelation 12:7-8)

The Divided Heaven.

One of Paradise.

One of the criminals who were hanged railed at him, saying, "Are you not the Christ? Save yourself and us!" But the other rebuked him, saying, "Do you not fear God, since you are under the same sentence of condemnation? And we indeed justly, for we are receiving the due reward of our deeds; but this man has done nothing wrong." And he said, **"Jesus, remember me when you come into your kingdom." And he said to him, "Truly, I say to you, today you will be with me in paradise."** (Luke 23:39-43; emphasis added)

I must go on boasting. Though there is nothing to be gained by it, I will go on to visions and revelations of the Lord. I know a man in Christ who fourteen years ago was caught up to the third heaven—whether in the body or out of the body I do not know, God knows. **And I know that this man was caught up into paradise**—whether in the body or out of the body I do not know, God knows—and he heard things that cannot be told, which man may not utter. (2 Corinthians 12:1-4; emphasis added)

Then the righteous will shine like the sun in the kingdom of their Father. He who has ears, let him hear. (Matthew 13:43)

He who has an ear, let him hear what the Spirit says to the churches. To the one who conquers I will grant to eat of the tree of life, which is in the paradise of God.' (Revelation 2:7)

I am the living bread that came down from heaven. If anyone eats of this bread, he will live forever. And the bread that I will give for the life of the world is my flesh." (John 6:51)

That whoever believes in him may have eternal life. (John 3:15)

Truly, truly, I say to you, whoever hears my word and believes him who sent me has eternal life. He does not come into judgment, but has passed from death to life. (John 5:24)

For I will be merciful toward their iniquities, and I will remember their sins no more." (Hebrews 8:12)

The poor man died and was carried by the angels to Abraham's side. (Luke 16:22a)

And one where Satan and his angels are currently allowed to continue:

[Thus, a portion of Heaven has sin still there.]

For we do not wrestle against flesh and blood, but against the rulers, against the authorities, **against the cosmic powers over this present darkness, against the spiritual forces of evil in the heavenly places**. (Ephesians 6:12; emphasis added)

So then, there will be a war one day in Heaven:

> Now war arose in heaven, Michael and his angels fighting against the dragon. And the dragon and his angels fought back, but he was defeated, and there was no longer any place for them in heaven. And the great dragon was thrown down, that ancient serpent, who is called the devil and Satan, the deceiver of the whole world—he was thrown down to the earth, and his angels were thrown down with him. (Revelation 12:7-9)

Leading to:

> And all who dwell on earth will worship it [the beast], everyone whose name <u>has not been written</u> before the foundation of the world in the book of life of the Lamb who was slain. (Revelation 13:8)

[With this, Heaven will become sinless once again, as with the New Earth.]

<u>Jesus's Second Coming.</u>

> And when he had said these things, as they were looking on, he was lifted up, and a cloud took him out of their sight. And while they were gazing into heaven as he went, behold, two men stood by them in white robes, and said, "Men of Galilee, why do you stand looking into heaven? This Jesus, who was taken up from you into heaven, will come in the same way as you saw him go into heaven." (Acts 1:9-11)

> Long ago, at many times and in many ways, God spoke to our fathers by the prophets, **but in these last days he has spoken to us by his Son,** whom he appointed the heir of

all things, **through whom also he created the world**. He is the radiance of the glory of God and the exact imprint of his nature, and he upholds the universe by the word of his power. After making purification for sins, he sat down at the right hand of the Majesty on high, having become as much superior to angels as the name he has inherited is more excellent than theirs. (Hebrews 1:1-4; emphasis added)

Yet it was the will of the LORD to crush him; he has put him to grief; when his soul makes an offering for guilt, he shall see his offspring; he shall prolong his days; the will of the LORD shall prosper in his hand. Out of the anguish of his soul he shall see and be satisfied; by his knowledge shall the righteous one, my servant, make many to be accounted righteous, and he shall bear their iniquities. Therefore I will divide him a portion with the many, and he shall divide the spoil with the strong, because he poured out his soul to death and was numbered with the transgressors; yet he bore the sin of many, and makes intercession for the transgressors. (Isaiah 53:10-12)

New Heavens, Earth and New Jerusalem.

"For behold, I create new heavens and a new earth, and the former things shall not be remembered or come into mind. (Isaiah 65:17)

But according to his promise we are waiting for new heavens and a new earth in which righteousness dwells. (2 Peter 3:13)

Of old you laid the foundation of the earth, and the heavens are the work of your hands. They will perish, but you will remain; <u>they will all wear out like a garment</u>. You will change them like a robe, and they will pass away, but you are the same, and your years have no end. The children of your servants shall dwell secure; their offspring shall be established before you. (Psalms 102:25-28; emphasis added)

But by the same word the heavens and earth that now exist are stored up for fire, being kept until the day of judgment and destruction of the ungodly. (2 Peter 3:7; emphasis added)

Then Peter said in reply, "See, we have left everything and followed you. What then will we have?" Jesus said to them, "Truly, I say to you, <u>in the new world</u>, **when the Son of Man will sit on his glorious throne,** you who have followed me will also sit on twelve thrones, judging the twelve tribes of Israel. And everyone who has left houses or brothers or sisters or father or mother or children or lands, for my name's sake, will receive a hundredfold and will inherit eternal life. But many who are first will be last, and the last first. (Matthew 19:27-30; emphasis added)

"For behold, I create new heavens and a new earth, and the former things shall not be remembered or come into mind. But be glad and rejoice forever in that which I create; for behold, I create Jerusalem to be a joy, and her people to be a gladness. I will rejoice in Jerusalem and be glad in my people; no more shall be heard in it the sound of weeping and the cry of distress. No more shall there be in it an infant who lives but a few days, or an old man who does not fill out his days, for the young man shall die a hundred years old, and the sinner a hundred years old shall be accursed. They shall build houses and inhabit them; they shall plant vineyards and eat their fruit. They shall not build and another inhabit; they shall not plant and another eat; for like the days of a tree shall the days of my people be, and my chosen shall long enjoy the work of their hands. They shall not labor in vain or bear children for calamity, for they shall be the offspring of the blessed of the LORD, and their descendants with them. Before they call I will answer; while they are yet speaking I will hear. The wolf and the lamb shall graze together; the lion shall eat straw like the ox, and dust shall be the serpent's food.

They shall not hurt or destroy in all my holy mountain," says the LORD. (Isaiah 65:17-25)

For as the new heavens and the new earth that I make shall remain before me, says the Lord, so shall your offspring and your name remain. (Isaiah 66:22)

Let this be recorded for a generation to come, **so that a people yet to be created may praise the LORD.** (Psalms 102:18; emphasis added)

But according to his promise we are waiting for new heavens and a new earth in which righteousness dwells. (2 Peter 3:13)

Then I saw a new heaven and a new earth, for the first heaven and the first earth had passed away, and the sea was no more ... He will wipe away every tear from their eyes, and death shall be no more, neither shall there be mourning, nor crying, nor pain anymore, for the former things have passed away. (Revelation 21:1, 4)

But what God foretold by the mouth of all the prophets, that his Christ would suffer, he thus fulfilled. Repent therefore, and turn back, that your sins may be blotted out, that times of refreshing may come from the presence of the Lord, and that he may **send the Christ appointed for you, Jesus, whom heaven must receive until the time for restoring all the things about which God spoke by the mouth of his holy prophets long ago.** (Acts 3:18-21; emphasis added)

I hope that you spent time studying these verses. I will now build the book around our birth and then our born-again life in Christ. A life lived in Jesus and He in us - leads to life with Jesus, on Earth, and as it will be in Heaven - all the stages of time that He has prepared for us to be face-to-face with Him - forever!

CHAPTER 1

Backgrounder

A Quick Overview to Set Us in Motion.

God created the Heavens and the Earth.
And God made all things. Everything. Seen and unseen.

Jesus at Creation.

And in view is Jesus, for

> **He is the image of the invisible God**, the firstborn of all creation. For <u>by him all things were created</u>, in heaven and on earth, visible and invisible, whether thrones or dominions or rulers or authorities—all things were created through him and for him. And he is before all things, and in him all things hold together. And he is the head of the body, the church. **He is the beginning**, the firstborn from the dead, that in everything he might be preeminent. For in him all the fullness of God was pleased to dwell, and through him to reconcile to himself all things, whether on earth or in heaven, making peace by the blood of his cross. (Colossians 1:15–20; emphasis added)

For God, who said, "Let light shine out of darkness," has shone in our hearts to give the light of the knowledge of the glory of God **in the face of Jesus Christ.** (2 Corinthians 4:6; emphasis added)

So as a reminder, Jesus is the one creating to the will of God the Father.

Earth.

And God formed the Earth, taking from the waters He first created.

And God said, "Let the waters under the heavens be gathered together into one place, and let the dry land appear." And it was so. God called the dry land Earth, and the waters that were gathered together he called Seas. And God saw that it was good. (Genesis 1:9–10)

He formed all the living plants.

And God said, "Let the earth sprout vegetation, plants yielding seed, and fruit trees bearing fruit in which is their seed, each according to its kind, on the earth." And it was so. The earth brought forth vegetation, plants yielding seed according to their own kinds, and trees bearing fruit in which is their seed, each according to its kind. And God saw that it was good. And there was evening and there was morning, the third day. (Genesis 1:11–13)

He formed the sun, moon, planets, and stars.

And God said, "Let there be lights in the expanse of the heavens to separate the day from the night. And let them be for signs and for seasons, and for days and years, and let them be lights in the expanse of the heavens to give light upon the earth." And it was so. And God made the two great lights—the greater light to rule the day and the lesser light to rule the night—and the stars. And God set them in the expanse of the heavens to give light on the earth, to rule over the day and over the night, and to separate the light from the darkness. And God saw that it was good. And there was evening and there was morning, the fourth day. (Genesis 1:14–19)

He formed all creatures big and small.

And God said, "Let the waters swarm with swarms of living creatures, and let birds fly above the earth across the expanse of the heavens." So God created the great sea creatures and every living creature that moves, with which the waters swarm, according to their kinds, and every winged bird according to its kind. And God saw that it was good. And God blessed them, saying, "Be fruitful and multiply and fill the waters in the seas, and let birds multiply on the earth." And there was evening and there was morning, the fifth day.

And God said, "Let the earth bring forth living creatures according to their kinds—livestock and creeping things and beasts of the earth according to their kinds." And it was so. And God made the beasts of the earth according to their kinds and the livestock according to their kinds, and everything that creeps on the ground according to its kind. And God saw that it was good. (Genesis 1:20–25)

And from the dust of the ground, God formed Adam, and the Spirit breathed life into him.

Then the LORD God formed the man of dust from the ground and breathed into his nostrils the breath of life, and the man became a living creature. (Genesis 2:7)

Now with this, God saw everything that He had made; and behold, it was good, and very good. And God placed Adam within the garden that God had planted. And God gave Adam the role of tending the garden. And within this garden, God placed two trees in the center of the garden.

The Tree of Knowledge of Good and Evil and the Tree of Life.

Note that God presented to Adam, and Adam later presented to Eve, the rule of God: not to eat the fruit of this one tree—the tree of knowledge of what is good and what is evil (sin). The pureness of God's instruction to not eat of this one tree was broken in disobedience by Adam and Eve and through the deceptive lies of Satan. And I cannot understand the desires of Adam and Eve's hearts to listen to the serpent in disobedience over God's presence and instruction. Also, note as the tree's name declares, "There is what is good, and there is what is evil." I'm postulating, but God calling everything good and very good gives me pause to say evil/sin came sometime after that. Creation was declared good by God. My supposition is that sin was somewhere too. I'm not smart enough to say when, where, why, or how sin came into the picture, but we know that Satan was a liar and murderer from the beginning (John 8:44). Now, where this falls within creation, I have no clue. However, God had within His will for sin to be. In His will, Jesus was to be and now is our Savior. So my conclusion is that God ordained sin to be present, and for a future day, Jesus will conquer all sin in heaven and earth. I don't know how and when sin came into play. Satan entered the garden through the snake after the tree of knowledge of good and evil was introduced to Adam and Eve. We know the outcome, but not the "how come."

God placed Adam in the garden as a caretaker and instructed Adam not to eat from the tree of knowledge of good and evil. It seems that this tree's fruit and the fruit from the tree of life held a unique purpose that God assigned, and maybe God's intent for those two trees was to guide the actions of Adam and Eve rather than serve as food. The other plants were for their eating, but these two trees had a central prominence within the garden and particular activities given to their fruit by God.

Therefore, God instructed Adam. He commanded Adam not to eat from the tree of knowledge of good and evil.

God said that if he did, Adam would die. (The wages of sin is death.)

God later put Adam to sleep, and from Adam's rib, He created Eve, Adam's wife and helper.

God communed with Adam and Eve, for God walked (remember, this is Jesus) in the garden where they lived.

Enter the serpent full of lies, deceptions, and death.

Two Observations.

1. God had placed the tree of knowledge of good and evil in the garden before He created Eve.
2. The serpent (the devil) appeared in the garden, presenting his sinfulness.

The serpent aimed to destroy what God called good. The snake was a liar and a deceiver.

The serpent persuaded Eve to disobey God's rule.

Adam and Eve, somewhere within themselves, had lust in their hearts and believed the serpent's lies; they took the fruit from the forbidden tree and sinned against God and His command.

They both ate the fruit.

And thus, sin within creation on earth was consummated.

God declared His righteousness.

God declared His punishment.

God declared His salvation toward Man.

Summary.

For your consideration, heaven and earth are in sin today. Satan and his angels sinned in heaven. Adam and Eve brought sin to Earth through Satan's lies about God and His commands and their lust to listen to another voice outside God's presence.

But God has a divine plan to send His only Son, Jesus Christ, to be the Savior of the World.

> Therefore, just as sin came into the world through one man, and death through sin, and so death spread to all men because all sinned— or sin indeed was in the world before the law was given, but sin is not counted where there is no law. Yet death reigned from Adam to Moses, even over those whose sinning was not like the transgression of Adam, who was a type of the one who was to come. But the free gift is not like the trespass. For if many died through one man's trespass, much more have the grace of God and the free gift by the grace of that one man Jesus Christ abounded for many. And the free gift is not like the result of that one man's sin. For the judgment following one trespass brought condemnation, but the free gift following many trespasses brought justification. For if, because of one man's trespass, death reigned through that one man, much more will those who receive the abundance of grace and the free

gift of righteousness reign in life through the one man Jesus Christ.

(Romans 5:12–17)

And God's plan of salvation was set before He created anything.

Blessed be the God and Father of our Lord Jesus Christ, *who has blessed us in Christ* <u>*with every spiritual blessing*</u> <u>*in the heavenly places*</u>, **even as he chose us in him** **before the foundation of the world**, that we should be holy and blameless before him. In love he predestined us for adoption to himself as sons through Jesus Christ, according to the purpose of his will, **to the praise of** **his glorious grace, with which he has blessed us in the** **Beloved.** In him we have redemption through his blood, the forgiveness of our trespasses, according to the riches of his grace, which he lavished upon us, in all wisdom and insight **making known to us the mystery of his will,** **according to his purpose, which he set forth in Christ as** **a plan for the fullness of time, to unite all things in him,** **things in heaven and things on earth.**

(Ephesians 1:3–10; emphasis added)

Heaven.

And God said, "Let there be an expanse in the midst of the waters, and let it separate the waters from the waters." And God made the expanse and separated the waters that were under the expanse from the waters that were above the expanse. And it was so. And God called the expanse

Heaven. And there was evening and there was morning, the second day.

(Genesis 1:6-8)

Now that God has created all things, let us explore what Scripture reveals about Heaven.

So, here are a few clarifications to note. Within the Bible, the heavens can refer to the galaxies of the sun, moon, and stars - as in verse 9. Or about the realm of the non-physical, as in a spiritual place, as declared in verse 8. For this study, my use is on Heaven, the latter when speaking generally.

It is the place where God currently resides.

Thus says the LORD: "Heaven is my throne, and the earth is my footstool.

(Isaiah 66:1a)

And Heaven is the place Jesus left to be born as a baby - to live a sinless life -and to die blameless at the hands of sinful humanity.

Have this mind among yourselves, which is yours in Christ Jesus, who, though he was in the form of God, did not count equality with God a thing to be grasped, but emptied himself, by taking the form of a servant, being born in the likeness of men. And being found in human form, he humbled himself by becoming obedient to the point of death, even death on a cross.

(Philippians 2:5-8)

And it is the same place that Jesus ascended to when He defeated death and the grave.

And when he had said these things, as they were looking on, he was lifted up, and a cloud took him out of their sight. And while they were gazing into heaven as he went, behold, two men stood by them in white robes, and said, "Men of Galilee, why do you stand looking into heaven? This Jesus, who was taken up from you into heaven, will come in the same way as you saw him go into heaven."

(Acts 1:9-11)

It is also the place where angels and other heavenly living beings reside.

In the year that King Uzziah died I saw the Lord sitting upon a throne, high and lifted up; and the train of his robe filled the temple. Above him stood the seraphim. Each had six wings: with two he covered his face, and with two he covered his feet, and with two he flew. And one called to another and said: "Holy, holy, holy is the LORD of hosts; the whole earth is full of his glory! **And the foundations of the thresholds shook at the voice of him who called, and the house was filled with smoke.**

(Isaiah 6:1-4; emphasis added)

It encompasses God's house, which has many rooms.

In my Father's house are many rooms. If it were not so, would I have told you that I go to prepare a place for you? And if I go and prepare a place for you, I will come again and will take you to myself, that where I am you may be also.

(John 14:2-3)

The Visual Appearance of Heaven.

The Bible offers a glimpse into some locations within Heaven. Such as God's throne room having what looks like precious metals and gems, as we know from what we have on earth, as told by the Old Testament prophets of Isaiah, Ezekiel, and New Testament Apostles of Paul and John.

It is also the place where the saints live in the presence of Jesus. And in this place, experience countless joys in Jesus. Jesus called it Paradise.

> And he said, "Jesus, remember me when you come into your kingdom." And he said to him, "Truly, I say to you, today you will be with me in paradise."
>
> (Luke 23:42-43)

A place that is restrictive to enter. The narrow door. [Jesus]

> "Enter by the narrow gate. For the gate is wide and the way is easy that leads to destruction, and those who enter by it are many. For the gate is narrow and the way is hard that leads to life, and those who find it are few.
>
> (Matthew 7:13-14)

> "Blessed are the poor in spirit, for theirs is the kingdom of heaven.
>
> (Matthew 5:3-12)

> "To you it has been given to know the secrets of the kingdom of heaven, but to them it has not been given.
>
> (Matthew 13:11)

Many references to different descriptive 'levels.' I.e., The Third Heaven.

I know a man in Christ who fourteen years ago was caught up to the third heaven—whether in the body or out of the body I do not know, God knows. And I know that this man was caught up into paradise—whether in the body or out of the body I do not know, God knows—

(2 Corinthians 12:2-3)

The Bifurcated Heaven.

You might wonder what I am saying when I say Heaven has two sides. Please allow me to present a few verses before I explain.

Blessed be the God and Father of our Lord Jesus Christ, who has blessed us in Christ with every spiritual **blessing in the heavenly places,**

(Ephesians 1:3; emphasis added)

For we do not wrestle against flesh and blood, but against the rulers, against the authorities, against the cosmic powers over this present darkness, **against the spiritual forces of evil in the heavenly places**.

(Ephesians 6:12; emphasis added)

Heaven appears to be divided into two parts. Spiritual blessings for the saints in Christ who currently live with Him in Heaven's paradise. They are experiencing eternal joy and a now always in the presence of Jesus. And then there is a place within Heaven where Satan and his angels reside. Where Satan and his minions stand before the Throne of God, accusing the saints on Earth. And where spiritual warfare with Satan and his fallen angels will go to battle against Michael and the angels of Glory. And he will be defeated! And he will be banished from Heaven -forever!

Now war arose in heaven, Michael and his angels fighting against the dragon. And the dragon and his angels fought back, **but he was defeated, and there was no longer any place for them in heaven.** And the great dragon was thrown down, that ancient serpent, who is called the devil and Satan, the deceiver of the whole world—he was thrown down to the earth, and his angels were thrown down with him. And I heard a loud voice in heaven, saying, "Now the salvation and the power and the kingdom of our God and the authority of his Christ have come, for **the accuser of our brothers has been thrown down, who accuses them day and night before our God.**

(Revelation 12:7-10; emphasis added)

And if a war, then sin is still present in Heaven.

And you were dead in the trespasses and sins in which you once walked, **following the course of this world, following <u>the prince of the power of the air</u>, the spirit that is now at work in the sons of disobedience—**

(Ephesians 2:1-2; emphasis added)

Thus, Satan is Still Inhabiting Heaven – for Now.

Heaven has a place where Satan and his minions 'reside' until he is cast out and thrown down to earth by the angel Michael for good - as scripture declared above. I see scripture pointing out that Satan today is before God - mainly within the Throne Room. I do not have biblical reasoning to understand that Satan and his fallen angels are permitted to be within the same area as the saints. All the saints have a perfect understanding [Hebrews 12:23c] and are now sinless and in paradise, as Ephesians 1:3 declares.

Therefore, if I understand scripture correctly, there is a place in Heaven where Satan is only allowed to be and not among the saints.

In Revelation 12:10, scripture declares that Satan stands before God in accusing the saints on earth.

Once Satan is ousted from Heaven and permitted time for his wrath to occur, Jesus will have him locked up in a pit for a thousand years. Afterward, he will be released for a short time and thrown into the Lake of Fire and Sulfur. Forever!

I am presenting once again for emphasis and understanding.

> For we do not wrestle against flesh and blood, but against the rulers, against the authorities, **against the cosmic powers over this present darkness, against** the spiritual forces of evil in the heavenly places.
>
> (Ephesians 6:12; emphasis added)

With that said, I also want to declare that by, through, in, and because of God's Spirit within us, we are children of Light – brought out from an evil, dark, sinful world.

> And even if our gospel is veiled, it is veiled to those who are perishing. In their case the god of this world has blinded the minds of the unbelievers, to keep them from seeing the light of the gospel of the glory of Christ, who is the image of God. For what we proclaim is not ourselves, but Jesus Christ as Lord, with ourselves as your servants for Jesus' sake. **For God, who said, "Let light shine out of darkness," has shone in our hearts to give the light of the knowledge of the glory of God in the face of Jesus Christ.**
>
> (2 Corinthians 4:3-6; emphasis added)

And from our salvation, the Holy Spirit who is in us, keeps us unto the day of either our death or Jesus' return, to be with us, and in us, as John 14 declares, not as orphans.

Therefore, Heaven is Corrupted by Sin.

Not by the saints in Heaven, who have been made righteous through Jesus and made perfect upon arriving.

> And **to the assembly of the firstborn who are enrolled in** Heaven [the saints who currently reside on Earth,] and to God, the judge of all, and **to the spirits of the righteous made perfect** [the saints who are currently residing in Heaven.]
>
> (Hebrews 12:23; emphasis added)

Heaven is not corrupted by the Heavenly host of God but by Satan and his minions.

So then, all creation is under the domain of sin [Romans 8:29] – but only to the point, God allows. To the time when Jesus puts all His enemies under His feet [1 Corinthians 15:26-28.]

Thus, all inhabitants of the world are under the curse of sin. In comparison, most of the inhabitants of heaven are sinless – again, sans Satan and his minions.

Hence, heaven is divided, with the whole earth under the curse of sin. "For all have sinned and fall short of the glory of God." (Romans 3:23)

> For **the creation** waits with eager longing for the revealing of the sons of God. For the creation was subjected to futility, not willingly, but because of him who subjected it, in hope that the creation itself will be set free from its bondage to corruption and obtain the freedom of the glory of the

children of God. For we know that the whole creation has been groaning together in the pains of childbirth until now. And not only the creation, but we ourselves, who have the firstfruits of the Spirit, groan inwardly as we wait eagerly for adoption as sons, the redemption of our bodies. For in this hope we were saved. Now hope that is seen is not hope. For who hopes for what he sees? But if we hope for what we do not see, we wait for it with patience.

(Romans 8:19-25; emphasis added)

The Future Eternity: New Heaven, New Earth, and New Jerusalem

For as in Adam all die, so also in Christ shall all be made alive. But each in his own order: Christ the firstfruits, then at his coming those who belong to Christ. Then comes the end, when he delivers the kingdom to God the Father after destroying every rule and every authority and power. For he must reign until he has put all his enemies under his feet. The last enemy to be destroyed is death. For "God has put all things in subjection under his feet." But when it says, "all things are put in subjection," it is plain that he is excepted who put all things in subjection under him. When all things are subjected to him, then the Son himself will also be subjected to him who put all things in subjection under him, that God may be all in all.

(1 Corinthians 15:22-28)

Of old you laid the foundation of the earth, and the heavens are the work of your hands. They will perish, but you will remain; they will all wear out like a garment. You will change them like a robe, and they will pass away, but you are the same, and your years have no end. The children of your servants shall dwell secure; their offspring shall be established before you.

(Psalms 102:25-28)

Then I saw a new heaven and a new earth, for the first heaven and the first earth had passed away, and the sea was no more. And I saw the holy city, new Jerusalem, coming down out of heaven from God, prepared as a bride adorned for her husband.

(Revelation 21:1-2)

Then Peter said in reply, "See, we have left everything and followed you. What then will we have?" Jesus said to them, "Truly, I say to you, in the new world, when the Son of Man will sit on his glorious throne, you who have followed me will also sit on twelve thrones, judging the twelve tribes of Israel. And everyone who has left houses or brothers or sisters or father or mother or children or lands, for my name's sake, will receive a hundredfold and will inherit eternal life. But many who are first will be last, and the last first.

(Matthew 19:27-30; emphasis added)

I call to your attention that Paul declares 'creation.' Not just the Earth but all creation groans because of sin. The scriptures I have quoted become the outline for this book and eternal life itself.

Jesus! Name above all names. Creator of all things! God of the Heavens and the Earth. King of Kings! Lord of Lords! Savior!

The Need for a Savior.

With sin having corrupted both Heaven and Earth. And with humanity under the curse of sin. And in God's will and purposes, it was always in the plan of God for Jesus to be our Lord and Savior.

> Long ago, at many times and in many ways, God spoke to our fathers by the prophets, but in these last days he has spoken to us by his Son, whom he appointed the heir of all things, through whom also he created the world. He is the radiance of the glory of God and the exact imprint of his nature, and he upholds the universe by the word of his power. After making purification for sins, he sat down at the right hand of the Majesty on high, having become as much superior to angels as the name he has inherited is more excellent than theirs.

> (Hebrews 1:1-4)

> Yet it was the will of the LORD to crush him; he has put him to grief; when his soul makes an offering for guilt, he shall see his offspring; he shall prolong his days; the will of the LORD shall prosper in his hand. Out of the anguish of his soul he shall see and be satisfied; by his knowledge shall the righteous one, my servant, make many to be accounted righteous, and he shall bear their iniquities. Therefore I will divide him a portion with the many, and he shall divide the spoil with the strong, because he poured out his soul to death and was numbered with the transgressors; yet he bore the sin of many, and makes intercession for the transgressors.

> (Isaiah 53:10-12)

Being revealed to us now is that there is a book written before creation. And the title of this book is 'The Book of Life of the Lamb who was Slain. And all who would believe are already written within this book.

> And all who dwell on earth will worship it [the beast, the antichrist], everyone whose name has not been written before the foundation of the world in the book of life of the Lamb who was slain.

(Revelation 13:8)

Therefore,

> The LORD says to my Lord: "Sit at my right hand, until I make your enemies your footstool."

(Psalms 110:1)

> Blessed be the God and Father of our Lord Jesus Christ, who has blessed us in Christ with every spiritual blessing in the heavenly places, even as he chose us in him before the foundation of the world, that we should be holy and blameless before him. In love he predestined us for adoption to himself as sons through Jesus Christ, according to the purpose of his will, to the praise of his glorious grace, with which he has blessed us in the Beloved. In him we have redemption through his blood, the forgiveness of our trespasses, according to the riches of his grace, which he lavished upon us, in all wisdom and insight making known to us the mystery of his will, according to his purpose, which he set forth in Christ as a plan for the fullness of time, to unite all things in him, things in heaven and things on earth.

(Ephesians 1:3-10; emphasis added)

For which Jesus prays:

> Father, I desire that they also, whom you have given me,
> may be with me where I am, to see my glory that you have
> given me because you loved me before the foundation of
> the world.

> (John 17:24)

> Then comes the end, when he delivers the kingdom to God
> the Father after destroying every rule and every authority
> and power. For he must reign until he has put all his
> enemies under his feet. The last enemy to be destroyed is
> death. For "God has put all things in subjection under his
> feet." But when it says, "all things are put in subjection," it
> is plain that he is excepted who put all things in subjection
> under him. When all things are subjected to him, then
> the Son himself will also be subjected to him who put all
> things in subjection under him, that God may be all in all.

> (1 Corinthians 15:24-28)

So now that I have presented the background and a quick overview of this
book, I pray that we are in one heart and Spirit, let us move forward to
study our heavenly call.

CHAPTER 2

Pressing Forward

Now that my wife Sandy has passed from life to life, I ask, what does death mean to a Christian? Of course, in my heart, I know that Sandy left her body as His child, and she immediately went 'home' to be with Jesus. But what does that entail?

Having died in our house, my darling wife left this world quickly. In retrospect, I remember having so many emotions when she died. I knew she had departed when I found her a few seconds later on the bathroom floor when I came rushing back into the bedroom that morning. My heart was racing, and I was sorrowful when I saw her, yet, I felt a divine calm over me at that moment, too. It is hard to put all the emotions racing within me. For being sad right then and there, for being helpless in trying to revive her when I found her on the floor a few seconds later, knowing that I wasn't in the room at the time when she left to be with Jesus – not having the opportunity to say 'I love you. Goodbye; see you soon.' My words to her were too late for her to hear me.

But I also felt a calming peace, for I can't explain what I felt this Monday morning that comforted me while waiting for the ambulance to arrive. For in my angst, I almost felt comforted too. For my family's sake, I'll skip the details of mom's passing that help explain the peace among the sadness, but say that my wife has finished the race – and finished well! She is now face-to-face with Jesus. Her faith is now complete. Having victory over sin in and through Jesus, now realized! Praise God!

Today, and as I write this with months now behind me, my grieving for the loss of my wife is gradually moving into fond memories of the time God gave us together. I feel drawn to writing about her new life in Heaven through the lens of the Bible. With the view from today - as I look to God's word for the future as what Sandy/Mom/Grammy is doing now - trusting that this study will offer comfort and hope to me, my family, and you, the reader—and now seeing the joy for a Christian moving into Heaven when our 'tents' fail.

Before I began, and as I finished writing the rough draft, I felt the Holy Spirit impress upon my heart to come back and bring Ephesians 1 to the lead position before I travel any further.

Blessed be the God and Father of our Lord Jesus Christ, who has blessed us in Christ *with every spiritual blessing in the heavenly places*, even as he chose us in him before the foundation of the world, that we should be holy and blameless before him. In love *he predestined us for adoption to himself as sons through Jesus Christ*, according to the purpose of his will, **to the praise of his glorious grace, with** which he has blessed us in the Beloved. In him we have redemption through his blood, the forgiveness of our trespasses, **according to the riches of his grace,** which he lavished upon us, in all wisdom and insight making known to us the mystery of his will, *according to his purpose,* which he set forth in Christ as a plan for the fullness of time, **to unite all things in him, things in heaven and things on earth.**

In him we have obtained an inheritance, having been predestined according to the purpose of him who works all things *according to the counsel of his will*, so that we who were the first to hope in Christ might be *to the praise of his glory.* In him you also, when you heard the word of truth, the gospel of your salvation, and believed in him, were *sealed with the promised Holy Spirit, who is the guarantee of our inheritance until we acquire possession of it, to the praise of his glory.*

(Ephesians 1:3-14; emphasis added)

[Key to the emphasis markings. First, read entire passage. Then read only shadowed highlights. Then read what is **bolded**, then underlined and lastly what is *italicized*. Notice how they connect in part as well as in total.]

Here before us are the promises of God towards us! These eleven verses hold a month of sermons! But, as they connect, they also have supportive verses in common. I've highlighted, underlined, and italicized points that stand in common for clarity and understanding of God's deep and wide promises. Read this as written, then go back and read what I have Underlined. Then go back and read just what I have emphasized in Bold. Then the Italics text. Etcetera. Finding the connective verses that Paul presents to us helps me see all the various nuggets of the promises we have in Christ! And then reread the whole quoted verses together and see how it pops!

So here are "The Questions I Ask."

CHAPTER 3

Saying Goodbye.

So, did my wife hear me say goodbye and that I loved her as she left her body and jumped into Heaven?

This question is a very problematic first question for me to ask. I would say no.

In my selfishness, I wanted her to hear my goodbyes, love for her, and heart for her. But I doubt that she heard me. She was already dead when I got to her.

As I searched the Bible for an answer, it is silent about those who have died. Do they hear the sounds and words of those left behind as they leave their bodies? Some who have died and then been resuscitated back to life have offered statements to the media about their experiences of being dead – like hovering over their bodies and seeing themselves leave their bodies. But would those experiences be real or like a dream? We just don't know. What happens at our last breath is our seeing Jesus instantly and not on those who remain behind; so the answer to my question, did she hear me say goodbye? I see within the Word of God the answer is no. And I have a strong reason as to why I say no.

Suddenly - is where the Bible gives detail. Paul writes about the moment of death:' we are absent from the body, and at home or present with the Lord.'

For while we are still in this tent, we groan, being burdened—not that we would be unclothed, but that we would be further clothed, so that what is mortal may be swallowed up by life. He who has prepared us for this very thing is God, who has given us the Spirit as a guarantee.

So we are always of good courage. We know that while we are at home in the body we are away from the Lord, for we walk by faith, not by sight. Yes, we are of good courage, and **we would rather be away from the body and at home with the Lord**.

(2 Corinthians 5:4-8; emphasis added)

When we go to Heaven, we go to Jesus. It is instantaneous. It's not a place we travel to - but arrive.

The Holy Spirit, who resides within those who believe, brings forth our spiritual bodies – swallowed up, as Paul declares – the instant this tent of a body ceases. And, in our new spiritual bodies, we are present before the Lord Jesus! Heaven is Jesus! Jesus is Heaven!

[Looking closer, Paul calls being away from our bodies upon death as being at home with Jesus. At home. For me, home means comfort, belonging, and where we began.

But our citizenship is in heaven, and from it we await a Savior, the Lord Jesus Christ,

(Philippians 3:20)

I realize that some readers may come from a broken home or didn't have a home. But know that when we are in Christ, we all have a home that does not compare to what we have on this earth.

When Jesus Raises the Dead.

There were zero testimonies within the Bible from those He brought back to life about what they saw, did, or understood about where they were. Their revival from the grave was for the Glory of God to be displayed. So in the moment of death, our body ceases to continue. Still, by and through the Holy Spirit, our saved spirit within us emerges and continues in life and is brought before our Lord and Savior, Jesus – now in our realized eternal life. Praise God!

As Jesus tells Nicodemus,

"Truly, truly, I say to you, unless one is born of water and the Spirit, he cannot enter the kingdom of God. That which is born of the flesh is flesh, and that which is born of the Spirit is spirit. Do not marvel that I said to you, 'You must be born again.'

(John 3:5-7)

Many folks look past these words of Jesus to Nicodemus. At best, they see the Holy Spirit's role in changing our hearts through grace and faith here on this earth, which is correct! Praise God!

But many may miss knowing that the Spirit's work also brings us into the Kingdom of God, Heaven. To believe is the work of the Holy Spirit changing our hearts and testifying to our spirit to the Gospel of Christ.

For God, who said, "Let light shine out of darkness," has shone in our hearts to give the light of the knowledge of the glory of God in the face of Jesus Christ.

(2 Corinthians 4:6)

> I will sprinkle clean water on you, and you shall be clean
> from all your uncleannesses, and from all your idols I will
> cleanse you. And I will give you a new heart, and a new
> spirit I will put within you. And I will remove the heart of
> stone from your flesh and give you a heart of flesh. And
> I will put my Spirit within you, and cause you to walk in
> my statutes and be careful to obey my rules.
>
> (Ezekiel 36:25-27)

But, the Holy Spirit is also our surety to the time of our last breath, and
He brings us into the Kingdom of God, transforming us from life to life.
Mortal bodies to spiritual bodies.

> And I will ask the Father, and he will give you another
> Helper, to be with you forever, even the Spirit of truth,
> whom the world cannot receive, because it neither sees
> him nor knows him. You know him, for he dwells with
> you and will be in you.
>
> (John 14:16-17)

> For we know that <u>if the tent that is our earthly home is</u>
> <u>destroyed,</u> <u>we have **a building from God, a house** not</u>
> <u>made with hands,</u> **eternal in the heavens.** For in this tent
> we groan, longing to put on our heavenly dwelling, if
> indeed by putting it on we may not be found naked. For
> while we are still in this tent, we groan, being burdened—
> not that we would be unclothed, but that we would be
> further clothed, **so that what is mortal may be swallowed**
> **up by life.** <u>He who has prepared us for this very thing is</u>
> <u>God, **who has given us the Spirit as a guarantee.**</u>

So we are always of good courage. We know that while we
are at home in the body we are away from the Lord, for we

walk by faith, not by sight. Yes, we are of good courage, and **we would rather be away from the body and at home with the Lord.**

(2 Corinthians 5:1-8; emphasis added)

I want to stop and make sure I am clear. My wife Sandy, your mother, your grandmother, and to the believer in Christ, your sister in Christ, had two birthdays. And for those of us who believe, we also have two births. For in our physical birth, God created us to be born through the union of our parents. Our being began in God's life-giving spirit, creating us [our soul] - manifested as flesh and blood at conception. So we celebrate every year and count the anniversaries of our physical birth, knowing that the counting will stop one day.

But God, in His glory and infinite wisdom, created us who believe in Him not for this world only, but for an eternity future, realized next in Heaven. Our second birth is spiritual. It comes through God by the Holy Spirit, birthing salvation in us. The Holy Spirit changes our hearts as we hear the Gospel - and we can now hear with understanding. And as God changes our hearts and our hearing of the Gospel makes sense to us, we repent and believe! With His Spirit changing our hearts, testifying to our spirit, and giving us His grace through faith - we become the "temple" of God, with the Holy Spirit living within us! Forever!

But if Christ is in you, although the body is dead because of sin, the Spirit is life because of righteousness. If the Spirit of him who raised Jesus from the dead dwells in you, he who raised Christ Jesus from the dead will also give life to your mortal bodies through his Spirit who dwells in you.

(Romans 8:10-11; emphasis added)

As Jesus rose from the dead, so shall it be for us who believe as we pass from this life to the next!

Jesus tells Nicodemus that. A believer's 'real' life is by the Spirit of God and begins at death, not birth.

> "Truly, truly, I say to you, unless one is born of water and the Spirit, he cannot enter the kingdom of God. That which is born of the flesh is flesh, and that which is born of the Spirit is spirit. Do not marvel that I said to you, 'You must be born again.'
>
> (John 3:5-7)

> Therefore, if anyone is in Christ, he is a new creation. The old has passed away; behold, the new has come. All this is from God, who through Christ reconciled us to himself
>
> (2 Corinthians 5:17-18a)

> Blessed be the God and Father of our Lord Jesus Christ! According to his great mercy, he has caused us to be born again to a living hope through the resurrection of Jesus Christ from the dead, to an inheritance that is imperishable, undefiled, and unfading, kept in heaven for you, who by God's power are being guarded through faith for a salvation ready to be revealed in the last time.
>
> (1 Peter 1:3-5)

Our salvation is a gift for, of, in, by, through, and because of God and His purposes - eternal purposes. All for His glory and our joy in Him!

The day of a believer's death is the day of realizing eternal life from our faith in Christ!

When my time comes, the joy of Jesus will outweigh the sorrow of those left behind. So, to answer the above question: it is absent from the body; present with the Lord. It is Born Again, now realized!

However, I know that God heard me tell Sandy goodbye. That I loved her deeply and that I will miss her. And I also know that God heard me praise Him for the time He gave us together. Again Lord. Thank you!

As you read this, you might question yourself about being born again, as Nicodemus did of Jesus, and wonder if you have had your second birth. If that is on your heart right now, the Holy Spirit might be actively drawing you to an understanding of the Gospel of Salvation. So what should you do - right now?

> For the wages of sin is death, but the free gift of God is eternal life in Christ Jesus our Lord.
>
> (Romans 6:23)

> But what does it say? "The word is near you, in your mouth and in your heart" (that is, the word of faith that we proclaim); because, if you confess with your mouth that Jesus is Lord and believe in your heart that God raised him from the dead, you will be saved. For with the heart one believes and is justified, and with the mouth one confesses and is saved. For the Scripture says, "Everyone who believes in him will not be put to shame." For there is no distinction between Jew and Greek; for the same Lord is Lord of all, bestowing his riches on all who call on him. For "everyone who calls on the name of the Lord will be saved."
>
> (Romans 10:8-13)

And if that just happened to you right now, and if you now understand the good news of Jesus as your Lord and Savior, you just became a child of God!

> But to all who did receive him, who believed in his name, he gave the right to become children of God, who were born, not of blood nor of the will of the flesh nor of the will of man, but of God.

(John 1:12-13)

SIDEBAR One: Peter Has the Keys?

So based on some denominational teachings, Peter holds the door to Heaven. So many humorous tells start, "there once were three folks who died, and they meet 'Saint Peter' upon their death …" I'll leave the joke there. But I don't think Peter is at Heaven's door, nor does he hold the entry keys.

First, let us look at what Jesus says to Peter and then at what Jesus means.

> Now when Jesus came into the district of Caesarea Philippi, he asked his disciples, "Who do people say that the Son of Man is?" And they said, "Some say John the Baptist, others say Elijah, and others Jeremiah or one of the prophets." He said to them, "But who do you say that I am?" Simon Peter replied, "You are the Christ, the Son of the living God." And Jesus answered him, "Blessed are you, Simon Bar-Jonah! For flesh and blood has not revealed this to you, but my Father who is in heaven. And I tell you, you are Peter, and on this rock I will build my church, and the gates of hell shall not prevail against it. I will give you the keys of the kingdom of heaven, and whatever you bind on earth shall be bound in heaven, and

whatever you loose on earth shall be loosed in heaven."
Then he strictly charged the disciples to tell no one that
he was the Christ.

(Matthew 16:13-20)

A few observations of value. Jesus asks his disciples, "who do people say that the Son of Man is"? Jesus is fishing. He was testing the waters on at least two fronts. First, what did the disciples hear about Himself in "the streets"? Which, by the way, Jesus knew.

And second, He was then testing His disciples by directing His question and applying it to HIMSELF. And, of course, the question and answer were not for Jesus' understanding but for the disciples' understanding.

Now see what Peter declares: "You are the Christ, the Son of the living God."

And then Jesus gives Peter a blessing, for He tells Peter that GOD the Father revealed this to you! God gave you the wisdom to know that Jesus is the Christ, the Son of the living God!

So with that, Jesus declares that either,

A. Because Peter knows the correct answer. Peter now holds the keys to the kingdom of Heaven, or
B. Peter (and now the other disciples) know that Jesus is the Son of Man, who is also the Christ, the Son of God, and that this understanding was given to them supernaturally by God the Father as they walked with God the Son. And in this understanding, Jesus declares the earthly mission He has prepared for them. Jesus was establishing the Church – moving from the synagogue to the Church through Peter and the other Disciples.

I chose B. For now, Jesus tells them and confirms that HE IS THE CHRIST! But then – tells them, "don't tell anyone." In my understanding of scripture, not yet.

I see Peter and the disciples holding the keys to the building of the Church and not directly to Heaven. And to the Church, to their testimonies after Jesus' resurrection. And by their testimony in the letters, they sent them to regional churches. So now, in total, the New Testament of the Bible.

Consider:

> "I do not ask for these only, but also **for those who will believe in me through their word,**

> (John 17:20 emphasis added)

> For we did not follow cleverly devised myths when we made known to you the power and coming of our Lord Jesus Christ, but we were eyewitnesses of his majesty. For when he received honor and glory from God the Father, and the voice was borne to him by the Majestic Glory, "This is my beloved Son, with whom I am well pleased," we ourselves heard this very voice borne from heaven, for we were with him on the holy mountain. **And we have the prophetic word more fully confirmed, to which you will do well to pay attention as to a lamp shining in a dark place, until the day dawns and the morning star rises in your hearts.**

> (2 Peter 1:16-19; emphasis added)

So when we breathe our last breath, we are present before Jesus. Peter, who precedes us, will be in Heaven. However, his role or reward will be in the New Jerusalem and not as Heaven's gatekeeper.

> It had a great, high wall, with twelve gates, and at the gates twelve angels, and on the gates the names of the twelve tribes of the sons of Israel were inscribed— on the east three gates, on the north three gates, on the south three gates, and on the west three gates. And the wall of the

city had twelve foundations, <u>and on them were the twelve names of the twelve apostles of the Lamb.</u>

(Revelation 21:12-14; emphasis added)

Then Peter said in reply, "See, we have left everything and followed you. What then will we have?" Jesus said to them, "Truly, I say to you, <u>in the new world</u>, when the Son of Man will sit on his glorious throne, <u>you who have followed me will also sit on twelve thrones, judging the twelve tribes of Israel.</u>

(Matthew 19:27-28; emphasis added)

CHAPTER 4

At Our Last Breath

So what happens at our last breath?

As we learned in the last chapter, we are absent from the body and present with the Lord when we die.

Will There Then - be Fear?

> Since therefore the children share in flesh and blood, he himself likewise partook of the same things, that through death he might destroy the one who has the power of death, that is, the devil, and deliver all those who through fear of death were subject to lifelong slavery.
>
> (Hebrews 2:14-15)

At one point, most Christians I know, myself included, feared dying.

However, we should know that we will never die because of Christ's finished work on the cross.

> Jesus said to her, "I am the resurrection and the life. Whoever believes in me, though he die, yet shall he live,

and <u>everyone who lives and believes in me shall never die</u>.
Do you believe this?"

(John 11:25-26; emphasis added)

For

Truly, truly, I say to you, whoever hears my word and
believes him who sent me has eternal life. He does not
come into judgment, but has passed from death to life.

(John 5:24)

We need to internalize that we are in Christ, and He is in us, and that, as
such, we never die!

But for some reason, we may allow ourselves to fall back into fear - whether
it is a resurgence of Covid-19, a terminal illness prognosis, or world unrest
knocking on the door. We may return to the fear of our demise even when
we have the assurance that being in Christ, we live forever – NOW and
FOREVER!

Or maybe it's not dying in and of itself, but perhaps the process of dying?

I wasn't in the room when my wife suffered a fatal heart attack. God spared
me from seeing her suddenly die.

Many of us worry about the 'how will I die.' Will it be long and painful
or short and quick? Or somewhere in between. Some folks say I want to
go quickly. Others say I want to know when my time is coming. Others
declare, 'take me as I sleep.' But, of course, we all have our thoughts about
what's best for us, agree?

In life, as God is sovereign in all life, every day has been given to us before
we are born:

35

> Your eyes saw my unformed substance; in your book were written, every one of them, the days that were formed for me, when as yet there was none of them.

> (Psalms 139:16)

And as Job realized:

> Since his [man's] days are determined, and the number of his months is with you, and you have appointed his limits that he cannot pass.

> (Job 14:5)

And to the day of one's death, God has that determined.

> No man has power to retain the spirit, or power over the day of death.

> (Ecclesiastes 8:8a)

But as believers in Christ, we know that Heaven is the place of our citizenship and that we are longing for the day God has planned for us to return;

> A good name is better than precious ointment, and the day of death than the day of birth.

> (Ecclesiastes 7:1)

And as the Apostle Paul writes:

> So we are always of good courage. We know that while we are at home in the body we are away from the Lord, for we walk by faith, not by sight. Yes, we are of good courage,

✦ *At Heaven's Door* ✦

and we would rather be away from the body and at home
with the Lord.

(2 Corinthians 5:6-8)

Therefore, when our time is moments away. Then, when the mission God
has given us is complete as to His plan for us; and then, after finishing the
walk in the good works that God has prepared for us to walk in:

> Moreover, it is required of stewards that they be found
> faithful.

(1 Corinthians 4:2)

As His Spirit is living within us and now united with our spirit – He gives
us eternal life. He opened our eyes and hearts to the truth of the Gospel the
day we first believed. Our walk in faith brings the fulfillment of salvation
when our body fails. God will usher us into His Heavenly Kingdom, and
we are in His presence as the Holy Spirit brings forth our spiritual bodies.
He is transforming the spirit of life He gave us at conception within
our mortal bodies into the eternal spiritual bodies of life before Him in
Heaven - upon our last breath. Like the outer shell of a seed pushed aside
from the inside, casting off the old surface of our mortal body through
the inner body bursting out from within, overtaking the old cover, and
growing, waiting for the time of the 'new plant' to emerge!

Steven's Homecoming.

One of the most incredible visual pictures of someone approaching their
transformation from life to life is Steven. And his body didn't fail in the
natural sense but was taken from him as Luke shares Steven's vision of his
entry into Jesus' presence.

> But he [Steven], full of the Holy Spirit, gazed into heaven
> and saw the glory of God, and Jesus standing at the right

hand of God. And he said, "Behold, I see the heavens opened, and the Son of Man standing at the right hand of God."

(Acts 7:55-56; emphasis added)

And as they were stoning Stephen, he called out, "Lord Jesus, receive my spirit." And falling to his knees he cried out with a loud voice, "Lord, do not hold this sin against them." And when he had said this, he fell asleep.

(Acts 7:59-60; emphasis added)

Take note that Steven called out to Jesus. And also note, Steven, declares, 'receive my spirit.' Absent from the body, present [in spirit] with the Lord Jesus.

In the Last Days, others will lose their lives for Christ's sake.

One other item to note regarding the timing of one's death -as with Steven, and as I present within my second book, En Route to the Mount of Olives, Matthew 24, some believers will also die for their testimony of Jesus. However, in the Last Days, there will be many whom God will call home through their testimony of Jesus during the tribulation.

Others will die at the hands of the antichrist and his helpers during the Great Tribulation.

Whether by age, illness, or violence, death for a believer funnels down to the last breath. This mortal body gives way to eternal life realized in the spiritual body that overtakes death, praising Jesus for His love and sacrifice for us. By His finished work of the cross, we believe that death brings life.

Getting to Our Last Breath.

Getting to our last breath may come suddenly or be seen as coming. But to those in Christ, Jesus will receive us in heaven with great joy. How we are called home might be hard for many of us to understand now. In part, Steven's account offers us an example of going to be with the Lord. He saw Jesus as he was transitioning from life to life.

Jesus greets us at the time He calls us home. Absent from the body, present with the Lord.

I believe with all my heart that my wife saw Jesus as her heart gave out. In the split second of her passing, Jesus revealed His love to us. He spared her the pain of suffering a prolonged death. Jesus also spared me the pain and memory of seeing her quick passing as she fell to the floor.

Absent From the Body; Present With the Lord.

And behold, I am with you always, to the end of the age."

(Matthew 28:20b)

Once again, this says it all.

CHAPTER 5

What did Sandy Experience Next?

When Sandy died that morning, can we know what she experienced – next?

Again, I suggest praising and adoring Jesus, her Lord and Savior.

So First Things First. Praise and Adoration.

I would speculate that now with perfect eyes, she would see herself in her spiritual body as she stood before our Lord and Savior.

As Bart Millard of MercyMe writes in "I Can Only Imagine," one of my wife's favorite songs, the lyrics speculate about dancing, standing, or kneeling before Jesus.

After all of life's struggles with sin, pain, and suffering, and now being before Jesus, being with Jesus would bring the fullness of unimaginable joy at first and everlasting sight! Seeing our Lord and Savior face-to-face and knowing and being known by Him would cause great emotion and celebration. Imagine seeing the Glory of Christ before her!

Now, with the actions of standing, kneeling, or dancing, I do not know how one would react. But in our home, we liked to hug as a sign of our love for each other.

As I wrote in my first book in chapter 17, I would like to have a hug from Jesus when I first see Him. But I know that seeing His glory will be so satisfying that that will be better than a hug.

For in fond remembrance, Sandy was a patter when she hugged. It was with her right hand behind your back when she hugged you, and she'd pat you five times. Not four, not six, but five times. Our family has a sweet memory of Mom's hugs that I share with you. When you received a hug from Sandy, you felt loved by her; even though the hugs were short and sweet - they were sincere.

And we made it a habit to hug at least every night, usually before we all went to bed. I miss that now with her. So having hugs every day showed and shared the love between us. So not that Sandy would hold Jesus with her right hand and pat Him five times, oh no. But maybe, just maybe, she melted within His arms as her love for Him was now realized, and she had the best hug ever.

Love. Hugs. Extremely important in life.

My Imagination.

And in my imagination, it would take me to look around next. So my hope for her is that she stood there, taking it all in next. Like going into a craft shop for her, Sandy enjoyed looking at all the supplies there. I loved watching her shop for crafting supplies. Watching her pick up and examine the materials and enjoy the yarns and other crafting supplies was my joy watching her! So in my heart of knowing her, and if God keeps our personalities in Heaven, as I believe He would, I say that she spent time taking in the Glory of God – and then, through time – stood in awe of her surroundings of Heaven proper - taking in the visuals of the kingdom! The other saints that are there! The Throne Room of God Almighty is before her! Those within His Court.

At once I was in the Spirit, and behold, a throne stood in heaven, with one seated on the throne. And he who sat there had the appearance of jasper and carnelian, and around the throne was a rainbow that had the appearance of an emerald. Around the throne were twenty-four thrones, and seated on the thrones were twenty-four elders, clothed in white garments, with golden crowns on their heads. From the throne came flashes of lightning, and rumblings and peals of thunder, and before the throne were burning seven torches of fire, which are the seven spirits of God, and before the throne there was as it were a sea of glass, like crystal.

And around the throne, on each side of the throne, are four living creatures, full of eyes in front and behind: the first living creature like a lion, the second living creature like an ox, the third living creature with the face of a man, and the fourth living creature like an eagle in flight. And the four living creatures, each of them with six wings, are full of eyes all around and within, and day and night they never cease to say,

"Holy, holy, holy, is the Lord God Almighty, who was and is and is to come!"

And whenever the living creatures give glory and honor and thanks to him who is seated on the throne, who lives forever and ever, the twenty-four elders fall down before him who is seated on the throne and worship him who lives forever and ever. They cast their crowns before the throne, saying,

"Worthy are you, our Lord and God, to receive glory and honor and power, for you created all things, and by your will they existed and were created."

(Revelation 4:2-11)

As believers in Jesus, we pass through this life on our way home to be with Jesus in Heaven next. Salvation is both the journey and the destination. Sandy, and for all who will believe, this life has its pain and its temporal joys. We are born into sin and, through God's grace in the faith that He gives us, calls us out of the world to run the race, finish, and finish well.

And given we will have perfect understandings in Heaven (Heb 12:23c), what joy I have for her in knowing all she has studied for within this life is complete. And all the fears, uncertainties, and doubts this life brings are gone. So now for her - and one day for us who would follow.

My heart pounds with excitement, knowing Sandy has arrived! She is no longer burdened by sin; in and through Christ, she now stands before Him and is in the pure joy of His Glory!

Then the righteous will shine like the sun in the kingdom of their Father. He who has ears, let him hear.

(Matthew 13:43)

Looking Through Sandy's Eyes.

As I was thinking about this for a moment, Sandy came to faith in Jesus as her Savior when she was thirteen. Over her life, God trained her by reading the Bible, attending decades of church and Sunday schools and youth groups, and participating with the Approved Workmen Are Not Ashamed (AWANA) Clubs - A kids' Church Ministry. And to all the times we spent together during our marriage of studying and praying together.

Sandy used what God gave her to serve others as a foundation for growth in her faith. And as I mentioned, she loved to craft. So Sandy used crafting as one of her ministries to people. She helped start a crafting guild that began as a church outreach many years ago. She loved making blankets and scarves and cross-stitched pictures for folks, usually with bible verses quoted within.

I found her scrapbooks with pictures of the crafts she had made for folks. So if you met Sandy for the first time and told her you were expecting a baby, you'd have a custom baby blanket at your door next week. She loved to craft; she loved giving.

She also worked in the nurseries at the churches we belonged to, and she helped in the kitchen and with church camps. And, of course, as our kids grew, we hosted church youth groups at our home.

Although my wife died in late November of 2021, she was about to finish her Christmas shopping. She so enjoyed giving gifts, and I supported her with her gift-giving, knowing that this was her calling through the gift of the Spirit.

And she would buy small gift cards for people she knew of but did not know, like the postal worker who delivered our mail.

Taking the faith that God gave her, Sandy ran with it. Good works DO NOT save a person. Good works are EVIDENCE that one is born of the Spirit in Christ [James 2:18}.

As Paul declares:

> But by the grace of God I am what I am, and his grace toward me was not in vain. On the contrary, I worked harder than any of them, though it was not I, but the grace of God that is with [in] me.

> (1 Corinthians 15:10)

And to the times of trials, tribulations, and testing that we experienced in life, Sandy endured by the grace and power of God.

November 29, 2021, was her graduation day. The work that God gave her to walk in is now complete. She finished. And, I would say, she finished well!

After forty-nine years of walking in His grace through faith, Sandy has now graduated. And is now face-to-face with Jesus! He's all that matters!

And so, too, it will be with us who also believe!

Seeing Jesus. Maybe dancing, standing, or kneeling before him, the moment of our last breath, as the song declares instantly before our Lord and Savior, Jesus!

We will see Jesus and now be with Jesus - forever! From life to life is the reward of God's grace through faith as we walk in the faith He has given us. The history of our past we bring with us will play a part in the time of Jesus' judgment.

CHAPTER 6

Life Places; Life Stages.

At this very moment, Sandy is in her new spiritual body, having passed from physical death to the realized spiritual life given to her when she first believed. She is also now with the ranks of the Heavenly saints, whom God calls to heaven when our mission on earth is complete.

Spiritual Body - A Secret and Hidden Wisdom of God Revealed through the Spirit.

Yet among the mature we do impart wisdom, although it is not a wisdom of this age or of the rulers of this age, who are doomed to pass away. But we impart a secret and hidden wisdom of God, which God decreed before the ages for our glory. None of the rulers of this age understood this, for if they had, they would not have crucified the Lord of glory. But, as it is written,

"What no eye has seen, nor ear heard, nor the heart of man imagined, what God has prepared for those who love him"— these things God has revealed to us through the Spirit. For the Spirit searches everything, even the depths of God. For who knows a person's thoughts except the spirit of that person, which is in him? So also no one comprehends the thoughts of God except the Spirit of God. Now we have received not the spirit of the world, but the Spirit who is from God, that we might understand the things freely given us by God. And we impart this in words not taught by human wisdom but taught by the Spirit, interpreting spiritual truths to those who are spiritual.

The natural person does not accept the things of the Spirit of God, for they are folly to him, and he is not able to understand them because they are spiritually discerned. The spiritual person judges all things, but is himself to be judged by no one. "For who has understood the mind of the Lord so as to instruct him?" **But we have the mind of Christ.**

(1 Corinthians 2:6-16; emphasis added)

'God has revealed to us through the Spirit.' As a believer in Christ, this is a supernatural work of God. For 'The natural person does not accept the things of the Spirit of God; for they are folly to him, and he cannot understand them, because they are spiritually discerned. The spiritual person judges all things.' So through the power of the Holy Spirit, He first saves us, now resides in us, and is our teacher of the precepts of God. He also moves us, secures us, and brings us from life to life, from this mortal tent of a body to the immortal building of a spiritual body. Salvation is all God's work in us and through us for His glory!

So is it with the resurrection of the dead. What is sown is perishable; what is raised is imperishable. It is sown in dishonor; it is raised in glory. It is sown in weakness; it is raised in power. It is sown a natural body; it is raised a spiritual body. If there is a natural body, there is also a spiritual body.

(1 Corinthians 15:42-44; emphasis added)

So this sparks more questions for me.

Life Places: Earth – Heaven – New Earth.

The next question deals with life locations. As we have learned, we are born on this earth and placed by God in the time and surroundings He has determined (Psalms 139:13-16; Acts 17:26). Then, when our life here is complete, God calls us home to Heaven, and we live with Him and Jesus and all the saints while Jesus is in Heaven.

> In my Father's house are many rooms. If it were not so, would I have told you that I go to prepare a place for you?
>
> (John 14:2)

> For God has not destined us for wrath, but to obtain salvation through our Lord Jesus Christ, who died for us **so that whether we are awake or asleep we might live with him**.
>
> (1 Thessalonians 5:9-10; emphasis added)

Jesus will return to earth to redeem all His sheep when God the Father says, go! For those whose bodies are 'asleep' in the ground and the sea – who are the saints in Heaven, and those who are alive in Him when He returns – who are those saints still living on this earth - will be caught up together by the angels. We will meet Him in the air (Matthew 24:31). Therefore, in His return, Jesus comes back to bring us together, to be with Him, and to judge the world. When Jesus returns, this also begins the wrath of God toward the earth and Satan himself, culminating in containing Satan for a thousand years and for Jesus to rule as Lord and King from this earth.

So God brings us all into existence through our parents' union at conception. We are born on this earth as sinners, both by birth and in our life deeds of sin. We then become saved when the Holy Spirit causes us to be born-again, to believe the Gospel of Christ - to the will of God the Father, as He had planned and ordained before He created anything.

"For God, who said,

"Let light shine out of darkness," has shone in our hearts to give the light of the knowledge of the glory of God in the face of Jesus Christ."

(2 Corinthians 4:5-6)

And now, " ...we are his workmanship, created in Christ Jesus for good works, which God prepared beforehand, that we should walk in them.

(Ephesians 2:10)

We all have been given a mission here on this earth to fulfill. And to those of faith, we now see His glory and know Him. And we have the purpose of seeking His will every moment of every day. Or at least that is what we should do. [See chapter 13 within my book 'The Sovereignty of God in Our Daily Lives.']

And then one day, as now, with my wife Sandy, when our time and missions are complete, God calls us home to Heaven. And it is in Heaven that we have our citizenship. So this residency in Heaven, as with the first earth, is only a 'layover.'

But our citizenship is in heaven, and from it we await a Savior, the Lord Jesus Christ, who will transform our lowly body to be like his glorious body, by the power that enables him even to subject all things to himself.

(Philippians 3:20-21)

When the time of this age is fulfilled as God had planned before He created it, this Heaven and Earth will pass away (Psalms 102:25-26), for God will present a new Heaven and a New Earth and a New Jerusalem as our eternal residence.

Therefore, this earth is our beginning. Heaven is where we transition next. And the New Earth at the end of the age is where we will live forever.

The next question deals with life experiences.

Life Stages: Perishable – Spiritual – Eternal.

Jesus is the Word of God (John 1:1), the ultimate Author of the Bible. The Bible tells us about life in and through Him through the Apostles and the Prophets. As believers in Christ, and if we make intentions to look, we see Jesus as the Author and finisher of our faith. We all go through times of life that God has set before us. But, as with places of residency, we also have stages of life experiences. And when I use the word experiences, we are not the masters of our domain; Jesus is.

Life stages can funnel down into two experiences for humanity. The first is towards those in Christ. Having Jesus within us is life! For Jesus declares He is the way, the truth, and the life! In our born-again experience, we have Jesus. He lives within us Now – and Forever!

The second experience is for those living outside of the salvation of Christ. For without Jesus, there is condemnation and death! And in death, eternal punishment, and separation. I hope and pray that the reader believes that Jesus is your Lord and Savior from sin!

So for us who believe, before the Rapture, our life stages have four significant events given to us by God. When we are born, and then, to the time and day, God causes us to be born-again, now not through parents, but through His Spirit, who changes our hearts and shines the glory of Christ within us. [Ezekiel 36:26-28, Hebrews 8:6-8, John 3:6, 1 John 3: 24]

Let us pause to highlight that physical birth is beyond our control and cognitive involvement. You and I are born to the actions and desires through the life of our parents. For God, He moves on and through the hearts of all to the council of His will. Even our parents' activities to the day of our conception, for our development and birth. Please understand that we have zero control over being born. In ignorance, we would today say thanks, mom and dad. But in wisdom, we would declare, thank you, God!

The action is similar to salvation, meaning God again has first involvement.

As with our birth, born-again comes through God's actions towards us. God creates us using mom and dad to give us life in physical birth. And in spiritual birth, God's Spirit brings us towards eternal life, to the moment of our cognitive understanding of the Gospel.

> - Jesus answered him, "Truly, truly, I say to you, unless one is born again he cannot see the kingdom of God." Nicodemus said to him, "How can a man be born when he is old? Can he enter a second time into his mother's womb and be born?" Jesus answered, "Truly, truly, I say to you, unless one is born of water and the Spirit, he cannot enter the kingdom of God. That which is born of the flesh is flesh, and that which is born of the Spirit is spirit. Do not marvel that I said to you, 'You must be born again.'
>
> (John 3:3-7)

Then, our reactions to both bring growth. In physical life, we become a product of our environment. In our spiritual life, we learn godly instruction through the Holy Spirit (I Corinthians 2;16). Everyone is born and learns. So too with us who believe. As God willed for us, we respond to God in birth [physical] and then in our second birth [spiritual].

Upon our last breath, the Spirit of God, who lives within us - instantly changes us from our mortal bodies into our spiritual bodies, and He then brings us directly to Jesus. Thus are being born again. From the day of our confession of faith - to now realized within the realm of Heaven!

And when Jesus one day returns to earth, we will be given our new resurrected immortal bodies, once again conjoined with our spiritual bodies [our spirit]. Not through birth, but again by God. And His Spirit and our spirit continue to live together inside our new bodies, and we have Christ in us, and we will also be with Jesus on the New Earth.

And, I see other scriptures declaring other salvation events and experiences beyond the Rapture to future believers birthed through the time of God's wrath as He brings judgment upon the world. But I will leave that for another time.

So to recap,

- The first life-stage event for a Christian has a mortal, physical body.
- The second life stage is being born again.
- When this body fails, it gives way to our eternal spiritual body.
- With Jesus' return to earth to redeem our bodies and judge the world, we will have a new, resurrected immortal body. And in the immortal body, the spiritual body dwells forever inside the new eternal body.

Mortal Body to Spiritual Body to Resurrected Body.

Our Spiritual bodies transition from within our Mortal bodies to one day into our Resurrected bodies. Perishable [Mortal], Spiritual, Immortal [Resurrected].

For example, when Jesus opens the fifth seal, John witnesses seeing people who died for their testimony of Jesus – who are now standing before God under the Alter of His Throne Room. The elder told him that these were the ones killed at the hands and direction of the antichrist during the Great Tribulation. This event occurs BEFORE the Rapture. They receive spiritual bodies and robes, and we see them waiting before God within His throne room. So as they are in Heaven, they know what happened to them, and they cry to God, when will you avenge our death (murder)?

Through the Great Tribulation and then to the Rapture, God has us in the 'time of the Gentiles.' This point will be critical to remember as we continue our studies.

Starting From Mortal to Spiritual.

Since we have the same spirit of faith according to what has been written, "I believed, and so I spoke," we also believe, and so we also speak, **knowing that he who raised the Lord Jesus will raise us also with Jesus and bring us with you into his presence.** For it is all for your sake, so that as grace extends to more and more people it may increase thanksgiving, **to the glory of God**

So we do not lose heart. **Though our outer self is wasting away, our inner self is being renewed day by day. For this light momentary affliction is preparing for us an eternal weight of glory beyond all comparison, as we look not to the things that are seen but to the things that are unseen. For the things that are seen are transient, but the things that are unseen are eternal.**

(2 Corinthians 4:13-18; emphasis added)

Therefore, with the Spirit of God who lives within us – and as He has raised to life the Lord Jesus, He will also raise us – to be with Jesus. And with the Spirit – He will bring us into His presence – transforming us into our spiritual body, a building made by God for us – to the glory of God.

Life begins at our conception - God had planned each of us before He created anything; thus, we begin life through a physical, sinful, mortal body. And this body that holds our spirit - saved by His Spirit - our life, this body, is seen by God as being only momentarily on this earth.

So, as God has ordained and planned for each of us before the foundation of the world, He brings us through this sinful world to the day He saves us in His Son Jesus, and He then prepares us through Christ for partaking in His eternal glory that can't even compare to this mortal life.

Faith, being the things unseen and hoped for, is eternally given by God's grace through faith by His indwelling Spirit. And with faith given by God, this is for the Glory of God, revealed to us as we pass through this life with our last breath into eternal life. So therefore:

> For **we know that if the tent that is our earthly home is destroyed, we have a building from God, a house not made with hands, eternal in the heavens.** <u>For in this tent we groan, longing to put on our heavenly dwelling,</u> if indeed by putting it on we may not be found naked.
>
> (2 Corinthians 5:1-3; emphasis added)

My thinking is that Paul is saying that being naked is a metaphor. Tents are a metaphor; naked is a metaphor. Being naked equates to not having clothes. Clothes are a covering. Tents cover—buildings house. We see many references to saints wearing white robes in Heaven, so I lean to say that not being naked means arriving saved and clothed in Christ's righteousness.

> **For while we are still in this tent, we groan, being burdened—not that we would be unclothed, but that we would be further clothed, so that what is mortal may be**

swallowed up by life. He who has prepared us for this very thing is God, <u>who has given us the Spirit as a guarantee</u>.

So we are always of good courage. We know that **while we are at home in the body we are away from the Lord, for we walk by faith,** <u>not by sight</u>. Yes, we are of good courage, and **we would rather be away from the body and at home with the Lord.** <u>So whether we are at home or away, we make it our aim to please him</u>. For we must all appear before the judgment seat of Christ, so that each one may receive what is due for what he has done in the body, whether good or evil.

(2 Corinthians 5:4-10; emphasis added)

Tents are, by nature, a temporary substitute for a house. Flimsy. Many tents are made from cloth. Offer little, if any, enduring durability. Paul was also a tentmaker. He knew all about tents and what function they served.

Then Spiritual to Immortal.

A tent was also the early meeting place where God presented Himself to Israel. When Jesus died, Jesus's payment for our sins, in part, ripped the curtain of the tent from top to bottom.

It was now about the sixth hour, and there was darkness over the whole land until the ninth hour, while the sun's light failed. **And the curtain of the temple was torn in two.** Then Jesus, calling out with a loud voice, said, "Father, into your hands I commit my spirit!" And having said this he breathed his last. Now when the centurion saw what had taken place, he praised God, saying, "Certainly this man was innocent!"

(Luke 23:44-47; emphasis added)

But when Christ appeared as a high priest of the good things that have come, **then through the greater and more perfect tent (not made with hands, that is, not of this creation)** he entered once for all into the holy places, not by means of the blood of goats and calves but by means of his own blood, thus securing an eternal redemption. For if the blood of goats and bulls, and the sprinkling of defiled persons with the ashes of a heifer, sanctify for the purification of the flesh, how much more will the blood of Christ, who through the eternal Spirit offered himself without blemish to God, purify our conscience from dead works to serve the living God.

Therefore he is the mediator of a new covenant, so that those who are called may receive the promised eternal inheritance, since a death has occurred that redeems them from the transgressions committed under the first covenant.

(Hebrews 9:11-15; emphasis added)

And did you catch the bold text? – 'more perfect tent,' 'Not made with hands,' i.e., 'not being of this creation.' Speaking to and of Jesus' resurrected body.

We are hitting the pause button again. Let us take in Jesus' life for a moment.

- Jesus is eternal.
- Jesus walked the garden in the cool of the day. Immortally in body, before He came to be born of a virgin!

- Then, as the prophets foretold, Jesus was born some 2,000 years ago.
- But Jesus was born sinless, whereas you and I were born in sin.
- Then Jesus lived life – entirely as a man – in the tent of His body - like you and me. He is 100% God and 100% man.
- Then Jesus was murdered, and I would say slaughtered for being sinless and killed by the world. And in His death, Jesus paid the price for our sins.
- Eternal Jesus, for a brief moment, He died - for us. He paid our price for our sins- so that we may live.
- Then Jesus gloriously arose! He cast off His mortal tent and put on His eternal resurrected immortal body.
- In summary, Jesus came to live on this earth. He was born a baby. Lived as a man - have a mortal, perishable body - a tent, like us. Yet perfect and sinless. Then, through Christ's death and HIS resurrection – which is the first fruit of the first resurrection, now – our tents – our mortal bodies, will put on immortality! Because of Jesus – we now are the first fruits of His Resurrection.

Let's continue.

God met with men like Abraham, Jacob, Isaac, Noah, and Moses one-on-one. Then, with and through Moses, God instructed Moses to construct a tent for God to be with His people. Later, David, but being implemented through Solomon, built the temple. Finally, God used King Cyrus to send Ezra and Nehemiah to reconstruct the second temple, with the temple centuries later suffering destruction. But with Jesus, the external temples were replaced because of the finished work of Jesus; and now every believer is the temple of God by the Holy Spirit's indwelling.

The metaphor is that our physically birthed bodies are like tents. Our salvation of being born-again comes during our lives on this earth. God causes our second birth to happen on the day in history He has declared it to be. We are being born-again - spiritually by His Spirit and in His Spirit.

Over time, our tents become weathered, torn, and beaten down - eventually useless as to the effects of sin upon them. God is sovereign in all things; His life plan for man's first birth was not for this mortal body to house our eternal permanence but, because of sin, a temporary covering. And I submit for consideration that this body is given for housing the spirit of a man. And when that tent finally fails for a Christian, God has prepared for us a building. Not temporal as a tent, but a building as in spirit. The idea is of strength and permanence, and not movable or weather-beaten. And as this tent is our earthly home, it is not – nor intended to be eternal. The building that God has waiting for us at our last breath, as guaranteed by and in the Holy Spirit, is presented to us at our last breath - is a spiritual body – a building, not another tent - not made with hands. But by God.

And because God, through His Spirit, lives within us who believe, our spiritual bodies will one day join with the immortal physical bodies that God also will give us at the First Resurrection - because of the finished work of Jesus! Praise God!

> These things God has revealed to us through the Spirit. For the Spirit searches everything, even the depths of God. For who knows a person's thoughts except the spirit of that person, which is in him? So also no one comprehends the thoughts of God except the Spirit of God. Now we have received not the spirit of the world, but the Spirit who is from God, that we might understand the things freely given us by God. And we impart this in words not taught by human wisdom but taught by the Spirit, interpreting spiritual truths to those who are spiritual.

> The natural person does not accept the things of the Spirit of God, for they are folly to him, and he is not able to understand them because they are spiritually discerned. The spiritual person judges all things, but is himself to be judged by no one. "For who has understood the mind

of the Lord so as to instruct him?" But we have the mind of Christ.

(1 Corinthians 2:10-16)

<u>You, however, are not in the flesh but in the Spirit</u>, if in fact the Spirit of God dwells in you. Anyone who does not have the Spirit of Christ does not belong to him. But if Christ is in you, although the body is dead because of sin, the Spirit is life because of righteousness. **If the Spirit of him who raised Jesus from the dead dwells in you, he who raised Christ Jesus from the dead will also give life to your mortal bodies through his Spirit who dwells in you**

(Romans 8:9-11; emphasis added)

And with the Holy Spirit within us, He is our guarantee in knowing that when the body dies or as our tent fails, we have a spiritual body waiting for us, clothed in Jesus' righteousness. So what is mortal will be swallowed up, replaced with –eternal life! - a living building that overtakes the mortal tent. And in and through faith, this is the lynchpin. Death is swallowed up in victory through the Cross of Christ by His resurrection from death! We are living in and through His righteousness! AMEN!

Mortal Body to Immortal Body. (The Rapture)

For this we declare to you by a word from the Lord, <u>that we who are alive, who are left until the coming of the Lord, will not precede those who have fallen asleep</u>. For the Lord himself will descend from heaven with a cry of command, with the voice of an archangel, and with the sound of the trumpet of God. And the dead in Christ will rise first. **Then we who are alive, who are left, will be caught up together with them in the clouds to meet the**

59

Lord in the air, and so we will always be with the Lord.
Therefore encourage one another with these words.

(1 Thessalonians 4:15-18; emphasis added)

As we are learning, a believer in Jesus has three life stages. And this is measured as having bodies.

I am repeating this for clarity and emphasis.

We are born with a physical body under the dominion of sin, age, death, and decay. And on the day of seeing the glory of Jesus and believing that He is our Lord and Savior through the Gospel, our spiritual birth happens.

The Spirit, who now lives inside this mortal body, helps us walk in the works of God that He has prepared for us to walk in. The Spirit works in us and through us in this mortal life, to the counsel of His will, and the Spirit is our surety to our eternal inheritance, bringing us to our spiritual body before Jesus, realized after our last breath. Being in Christ, and He in us, His Spirit continues living in us now as part of us; when the end of the age of the world comes, our spiritual body dwells within our raptured bodies, which God gives us as immortal, imperishable, eternal.

SIDEBAR Two – Jesus within Us.

But if Christ is in you, although the body is dead because of sin, the Spirit is life because of righteousness.

(Romans 8:10; emphasis added)

[Please take note. Jesus and the Father are One. Jesus and the Holy Spirit are One! The Holy Spirit living within us is the same as Christ living in us [Galatians 2:12]! Jesus is the manifestation of God the Father and God the Spirit! Therefore, Jesus is alive, now, and in all who believe!]

At the time of the Rapture.

However, at the Rapture, I see something different for believers alive on earth. There will be a jumping over the spiritual body given to believers and move right into their new, immortal bodies God has prepared for all believers at the time of Jesus' return. So for these believers, they go from mortal to immortal bodies - skipping over the spiritual body that those before the Rapture received when they entered Heaven.

The Holy Spirit is always with and in us who believe, so those alive will still have His presence within them.

> And I will ask the Father, and he will give you another Helper, **to be with you forever**, even the Spirit of truth, whom the world cannot receive, because it neither sees him nor knows him. You know him, for **he dwells with you and will be in you.**
>
> (John 14:16-17; emphasis added)

They will see Jesus coming in the clouds, as they are called upward to meet Him.

> Then we who are alive, who are left, will be caught up together with them in the clouds to meet the Lord in the air, and so we will always be with the Lord.
>
> (1 Thessalonians 4:17; emphasis added)

The whole world will see Jesus coming too. But they will be fearful and try to hide.

> "Immediately after the tribulation of those days the sun will be darkened, and the moon will not give its light, and the stars will fall from heaven, and the powers of the heavens will be shaken. Then will appear in heaven the

sign of the Son of Man, and then all the tribes of the earth will mourn, **and they will see the Son of Man coming on the clouds of heaven with power and great glory. And he will send out his angels with a loud trumpet call, and they will gather his elect** from the four winds, from one end of heaven to the other.

(Matthew 24:29-31; emphasis added)

At the rapture, "Then we who are alive, who are left, will be caught up together with them in the clouds to meet the Lord in the air; and so we will always be with the Lord.."

Three life experiences for those who are alive on earth when Jesus returns..

- Physical Birth
- Born Again
- Resurrected bodies.

CHAPTER 7

Is it Possible to Know...

As I arrived at Chapter Seven, I needed to shorten my question list. So as I was studying to address the first six chapters, my studies drove me to ask more questions. More questions than I first realized I had within me. The beauty of studying God's word - the richness of the time spent with Him through His Spirit, in His word - brings joy in getting closer to Him. And as I was noting the new questions I now had, I thought the book had the potential of never getting finished. So I realized I needed to slow down and put a hold on the new questions. So in outline format. Here are the questions I will present to you - next.

- Is there community in Heaven
- What is life like in Heaven?
- Is it possible to describe the appearance of Heaven?
- What did Jesus mean within John 14?
- On Earth, in Heaven? [Physical then Spiritual]
- That we will be known?
- Will we have or maintain our emotions?
- Can those in Heaven see those of us who remain on Earth?
- Every Family in Heaven and on Earth.
- What about our earthly families now in Heaven with us?
- In Heaven, will we retain new memories/experiences?
- Is entry into Heaven limited?
- Will we one day forget our past, i.e., as we live on the New Earth?

Is There Community in Heaven and if so, What is Life Like in Heaven?

> "Let not your hearts be troubled. Believe in God; believe also in me. **In my Father's house are many rooms.** If it were not so, would I have told you that I go to prepare a place for you? And if I go and prepare a place for you, I will come again and will take you to myself, that where I am you may be also. **And you know the way to where I am going.**" Thomas said to him, "Lord, we do not know where you are going. How can we know the way?" Jesus said to him, "I am the way, and the truth, and the life. No one comes to the Father except through me. If you had known me, you would have known my Father also. From now on you do know him and have seen him."
>
> (John 14:1-7; emphasis added)

As I shared earlier, my wife loved to craft. So when we first entered our sixties, we would always tease each other about a future time into our eighties about needing physical support. And if she then needed to go into assisted living, she would tell the family - give her enough yarn and cross-stitching material, and she'd be happy.

So this leads to a mixture of questions. What will life in Heaven hold for us? What will we do? And so much more.

Heaven is Life Eternal with Jesus.

Life with Jesus. As mentioned in answers to my other questions, we see many rooms and possibly something of a city in Heaven. Maybe even the New Jerusalem is currently there?

> And I saw the holy city, **new Jerusalem**, coming down
> out of heaven from God, prepared as a bride adorned for
> her husband.
>
> (Revelation 21:2; emphasis added)

As with the actions and activities on earth today, life in Heaven will also have constant activities. However, there will be perfect understanding and great joy in Jesus.

> But, as it is written, "What no eye has seen, nor ear heard,
> nor the heart of man imagined, what God has prepared
> for those who love him"—
>
> (1 Corinthians 2:9)

We do know that there will be times of worship. I imagine it could be like the church here on earth—a set time to gather. And yes, there is time in Heaven. When Jesus opens the 7th seal, John declares there was silence in Heaven for about half an hour.

As God has set the Sabbath after creation for man to observe, I think it would be similar within Heaven. We see that God has a Throne Room and that those who died within the Great Tribulation are standing before Him as they meet with God. So my next question is, 'where are the other saints who live in Heaven during this moment in the future as given to John to witness?' I suggest that they are somewhere else during this event.

I'd also think there would be a great reunion. Scripturally, I have little support for the details of what occurs in this. But God created us as social beings here on this earth.

As I authored this book, I experienced the passing of my last aunt and a few friends. All who professed their life in Jesus. So I am sure that they, too, are face to face with Jesus, and I would imagine that Sandy and others greeted them at some point.

And if I were to further ponder as to all the Heavenly reunions that occur, I hope that they will fondly remember all the relationships of their mutual past, AND, in praise to the Lord, would rejoice and be glad.

So as we are encouraged to gather together, worship God, and pray together here on this earth, I cannot imagine it any different in Heaven.

> And let us consider how to stir up one another to love and good works, not neglecting to meet together, as is the habit of some, but encouraging one another, and all the more as you see the Day drawing near.
>
> (Hebrews 10:24-25)

Again, the difference is that all the saints of heaven are now in their Heavenly [spiritual] bodies. Being made perfect and living in paradise, life now lived in perfection. So I would perceive that the physical world that our Lord has created would no longer be of any significance to their life in heaven. However, the memory of our lives lived in this world will be retained and enhanced in detail. But for now, being made perfect, my heart would think that in all memories of this life, we would praise Jesus for His forgiveness in times of sin. Or to the glory for the time of His protection from evil [Jude 24-25]. Or for praises to the times of His workings within us and the answers to our prayers on Earth.

And as a brief aside, I would also imagine that sleeping is no longer a requirement once in heaven - as with eating. Instead, the Glory of Christ would shine continually, just as He would when He returns to Earth.

My heart again would point to having 100% joy, and, to use an earthen term, having joy 24 x7, for all the saints of heaven are in the community before Jesus.

And I believe I can take the liberty through the word to say this, for Jesus shares that Abraham and Lazarus are socializing together in heaven.

The poor man died and was carried by the angels to Abraham's side.

(Luke 16:22a)

So in my mind, I would think that all the prayers we offer to God have eternal importance. In our prayers while on this earth, I imagine the saints in Heaven would recall those prayers. They are now offering praise and thanksgiving to the Glory of God for His work within those prayers. And would praise God for His answering the salvation call of others through their prayers now remembered in Heaven.

As an example, Sandy and I have prayed for our children for God to save them. And we prayed frequently. And that my parents, who are also in Heaven, also prayed for our children while living on this earth. And with that, they are now praising Jesus for answering those prayers and giving Him the glory for saving them. And we also prayed, and I continue to pray for our grandchildren.

Or to our prayers praying for the needs of others on their behalf, for God's actions; or of the prayers answered through God's miracles in healings, blessings, and His glory to be on display! As a community living in Heaven, there is no isolation. I imagine those in Heaven now having perfect understanding will relate and testify to God's goodness. Abraham and Lazarus live together and know each other, and the history of their lives on earth gives us insight into community relationships in Heaven, as Jesus shares in Luke 16.

God covets our prayers, and He also keeps them.

And when he had taken the scroll, the four living creatures and the twenty-four elders fell down before the Lamb, each holding a harp, and golden bowls full of incense, which are the prayers of the saints

(Revelation 5:8)

Now remember, once in Heaven, we are made perfect, so our prayer life while on this Earth turns into pure praise and adoration when we enter Jesus' presence. So my wife is not praying for me while in Heaven, but praising God for the time of life He gave her on Earth and the past events she experienced. And would further postulate that she will be praising God for her time here as my wife, mother, daughter, sister, grandmother, friend, etc.

Conversely, there is no need for me to continue to pray for her, for she is now complete and is before Jesus.

And there is no biblical foundation to pray for the dead. Nor is there purgatory or a transitory state. And there is no soul sleep. Or a foundation to pray to anyone except God the Father, Son, and Spirit. Jesus is our advocate in all of our prayers.

Thus we know that those who die in Jesus are instantly before Him. Amen!

So know that God is the God of the living! And in knowing this truth, Sandy and all the saints in Heaven are in the community of Heaven.

And because of community, my heart says that Heaven will have social gatherings. But I don't think there will be crafting or sports rooms. But maybe on the new Earth? But we will all find out one day for sure.

And, of course, we will be singing praises!

Oh, how magnificent the choir will be! Oh, how everyone will sing as they have never sung before! And in my opinion, in perfect pitch and at the ideal time. Jesus is worthy! And our hearts will explode in praise, love, and glory for our Lord and Savior!

Sights, Sounds, Smells

Just another quick observation. Our senses, along with our emotions, continue in Heaven.

We will have our vision. We will also have our hearing. And we will be able to talk with each other. And the songs of praise we will sing. And we will still have the ability to hold and touch. And we will retain the sense of smell. But to taste, eating seems to be the activity of the physical world.

Jesus states: And when the hour came, he reclined at the table and the apostles with him. And he said to them, "I have earnestly desired to eat this Passover with you before I suffer. For I tell you I will not eat it until it is fulfilled in the kingdom of God." Luke 22:14-16.

We are who God has created us to be and are in the personalities and traits He has uniquely given us. As when on this Earth, we manifest sinlessness in Heaven, so my memory of Sandy and my love for her will never grow old and fade away. For in Heaven, we will remember the time of this life we shared, but with full awareness. Now, not as married in Heaven. But in remembrance, as having been married on this Earth.

And if you have been married to more than one person in this world, you will also retain that memory. But as I mentioned above, we will give all glory to Jesus. The good and the bad of this life lived. So you would thank Jesus for forgiveness and blessing throughout your life.

What Does Heaven look like?

As I shared within Chapter One, the throne room of God has many descriptors, looking like gold and precious gems.

> After this I looked, and behold, a door standing open in heaven! And the first voice, which I had heard speaking to me like a trumpet, said, "Come up here, and I will show you what must take place after this." At once I

was in the Spirit, and behold, a throne stood in heaven,
with one seated on the throne. And he who sat there
had the appearance of jasper and carnelian, and around
the throne was a rainbow that had the appearance of an
emerald. Around the throne were twenty-four thrones,
and seated on the thrones were twenty-four elders, clothed
in white garments, with golden crowns on their heads.
From the throne came flashes of lightning, and rumblings
and peals of thunder, and before the throne were burning
seven torches of fire, which are the seven spirits of God,
and before the throne there was as it were a sea of glass,
like crystal.

(Revelation 4:1-6)

There are many rooms within the Father's house.

In my Father's house are many rooms. If it were not so,
would I have told you that I go to prepare a place for you?
And if I go and prepare a place for you, I will come again
and will take you to myself, that where I am you may be
also.

(John 14:2-3; emphasis added)

In the context of the text within the Bible, it declares that Heaven will have
at least God's house and many rooms. And within the Father's house, there
is His throne room. Maybe there are other cities and other homes? Maybe?

Paul, five times within his letter to the Ephesians, speaks of Heavenly
places. Places.

Blessed be the God and Father of our Lord Jesus Christ, who has blessed us in Christ with every spiritual blessing in the heavenly places,

(Ephesians 1:3; emphasis added)

That he worked in Christ when he raised him from the dead and seated him at his right hand in the heavenly places, far above all rule and authority and power and dominion, and above every name that is named, not only in this age but also in the one to come.

(Ephesians 1:20-21; emphasis added)

But God, being rich in mercy, because of the great love with which he loved us, even when we were dead in our trespasses, made us alive together with Christ— by grace you have been saved— and raised us up with him and seated us with him in the heavenly places in Christ Jesus, so that in the coming ages he might show the immeasurable riches of his grace in kindness toward us in Christ Jesus.

(Ephesians 2:4-7; emphasis added)

And to bring to light for everyone what is the plan of the mystery hidden for ages in God, who created all things, so that through the church the manifold wisdom of God might now be made known to the rulers and authorities in the heavenly places. This was according to the eternal purpose that he has realized in Christ Jesus our Lord, in whom we have boldness and access with confidence through our faith in him.

(Ephesians 3:9-12; emphasis added)

And as I previously shared and will further present to you that Heaven has division. Into parts of separation between Good and Evil.

> For we do not wrestle against flesh and blood, but against the rulers, against the authorities, against the cosmic powers over this present darkness, against the spiritual forces of evil in the heavenly places.
>
> (Ephesians 6:12; emphasis added)

Heaven. God's house is there. He has a throne room. His house has many rooms. There are places. And the New Jerusalem descends from Heaven to the New Earth. So there is a high probability that there are cities.

Rabbit Trail One: John 14.

As I read the last quote from John 14 and the rooms within the Father's house, I'm drawn into the text to understand what Jesus is saying.

Jesus says that His Father's house has many rooms.

Then Jesus says that HE will prepare a place for you [disciples – now us.]

And further, He declares that He will come again – AND – and 'take you to Me.'

Why? So that where Jesus is, you [we] may also be.

The where doesn't fit the Father's rooms, nor the place that Jesus prepares per se, but unto Himself!

So is this a reference to the second coming? The rapture? Death? Or life now!

Again, for your consideration, Jesus is telling us that it is He - who is THE place, for He is going to the Cross – very soon. Jesus is the door to the rooms He is preparing - and is now ready for us- through the His finished work of the Cross. John Piper says it best.

> "'And if I go and prepare a place for you, I will come again and will take you to myself, that where I am you may be also.'
>
> I think this is one of the most important phrases in this passage: I will take you to myself. This shifts the focus from a place to a person. Where Jesus is, there is heaven. What is the essence of heaven? The immediate presence of Jesus. So when he says, "I go to prepare a place for you," isn't the essence of what he is saying, "I go this night through death for you, and I go Easter Sunday morning out of death for you, so that I myself might be your living dwelling place"?
>
> I am your room in my Father's house. And I am not yet prepared to receive you there. I must die. I must rise. I must be glorified. I must intercede for you. And when I have done that, then I will be ready. I will come and take you to myself.
>
> Don't use this passage of Scripture to show that when Jesus comes back at the second coming he will take you to heaven. It does not say that. It says, "I will come again and will take you to myself, that where I am you may be also." And where will he be when he comes? We will meet him in the air, and he will establish his reign on the earth. And so we will forever be with the Lord (1 Thessalonians 4:16–17).
>
> What this text focuses on in the second coming is not a return to heaven but a reunion with Christ. "I will come again and will take you to myself." Therefore, my beloved

disciples, let not your heart be troubled. Trust. Trust me that I am coming for you. I will come. I will take you. And trust me because the dwelling I have prepared for you is my crucified, risen, and glorified self. Don't be troubled, I will come and take you to myself."

John Piper https://www.desiringgod.org/messages/i-am-the-way-the-truth-and-the-life, March 23, 20122. Pulled on March 28, 2022

Heaven is Jesus. Jesus is Heaven.

Heaven, in many ways, is also another 'world.'

Heaven has many places. And possibly New Jerusalem is currently there. We have seen through the Bible that God has His house, which has uncountable rooms. As we previously noted, God also has meeting areas. As one, God's throne room.

The other point to note is when Jesus declares that there are many rooms in the house of God. Here is where my mind wanders a bit. Will the rooms be like a college dormitory, where each person occupies 'their room' in 'downtime?' And is there downtime?

As the old hymn writers declare, will those rooms be mansions?

Having rooms for all the saints somewhat intrigues me, for does this indicate some personal Heavenly real estate for all the saints to reside? And what I mean by real estate is it a place assigned to be where, if, and when, not collectively together?

And then, what is in every room? I can't imagine furniture, a bed, or a TV, but something must happen in these rooms, for Jesus declares that there are many rooms. So having personal space for all the saints, as I also imagine, must be in unlimited supply.

But then again, God has a throne, and Jesus is seated on the right hand of God, the father. So maybe there will be furniture? [Which begs another question. We will all be wearing white robes. Who makes these robes? Oh, the rabbit trails!]

And then, when are we in those rooms? Is there a time that would cause us to retreat to 'our rooms' as we would on earth?' And what would cause us to leave those rooms, and when would we leave those rooms?

Are the rooms big enough to host guests? Since we are all together in the Glory of Christ, how would our rooms be collectively received? And would we be able to host visitors? And if so, will we be able to invite Jesus into our room, as He visited our homes here on earth? Oh my! The questions from my limited understanding of my life experiences on earth can wander endlessly.

Heaven is the current place of residence for the saints. But Heaven is not the place in focus, nor is our room, for Jesus is the person of emphasis! So looking at Jesus, looking to Jesus, being in Jesus, Jesus in us - is Heaven realized!

Sandy is before Jesus! She is in Heaven! Imagine the Glory of God is before her and the joy she has –forever!

Jesus is Heaven!

That We Will Be Known? Luke 16

Will our names follow us into Heaven? Will our deeds on earth be remembered? Will we be known as being from our families? Forever by our name? Will we still be social with other believers too?

As I started to share, the answer was yes.

When Jesus shared the story of Lazarus and the rich man, Lazarus was with Abraham.

> "There was a rich man who was clothed in purple and fine linen and who feasted sumptuously every day. And at his gate was laid a poor man named Lazarus, covered with sores, who desired to be fed with what fell from the rich man's table. Moreover, even the dogs came and licked his sores. The poor man died and was carried by the angels to Abraham's side. The rich man also died and was buried, and in Hades, being in torment, he lifted up his eyes and **saw Abraham far off and Lazarus at his side.**

> (Luke 16:19-23; emphasis added)

I am using this story Jesus told in support of answering many of my questions. As I read this, I do not understand this as a parable that Jesus tells us but as a life event that happened, starting on earth and culminating in Heaven. We know Abraham, for the rich man called him Father Abraham. Knowing that Abraham lived in world history, Jesus tells us something that has happened or will happen in Heaven.

In this snippet of life in Heaven, we see three people: the rich man, Lazarus, and Abraham. For the questions I raise about Heaven and knowing others in Heaven, Jesus tells us that Lazarus and Abraham were together. And they know each other, and they are now with each other. And they also know the rich man. And what his earthly life was also like. And that he is residing in Hades.

Jesus continues:

> And he called out, Father Abraham, have mercy on me, and send Lazarus to dip the end of his finger in water and cool my tongue, for I am in anguish in this flame.' But Abraham said, 'Child, **remember** that you in your

lifetime received your good things, and Lazarus in like manner bad things; but now he is comforted here, and you are in anguish. And besides all this, **between us** and you a great chasm has been fixed, in order that those who would pass from here to you may not be able, and none may cross from there to **us.**'

(Luke 16:24-26; emphasis added)

Us. So confirming, there is an us. When we enter the presence of Jesus in Heaven, we are all known for who we are. And in being known by our names, we will also know others. We are also known for what we did in our lifetimes. So Jesus declares to us, within Luke 16, the lives of Abraham, Lazarus, and the rich man from their time in the world.

So then you are no longer strangers and aliens, but you are **fellow citizens with the saints and members of the household of God,** built on the foundation of the apostles and prophets, Christ Jesus himself being the cornerstone, in whom **the whole structure, being joined together, grows into a holy temple in the Lord In him** you also are being built together into a dwelling place for God by the Spirit.

(Ephesians 2:19-22; emphasis added)

For the saints, my heart would say that for all the good works God has given us to walk in (Ephesians 2:10), we will praise Him for what He has done in and through our lives.

And for the sins that we did – I believe that we will remember them; however, we will praise Jesus in His forgiveness of those sins on earth (Luke 5:20). The focus of remembrance will be praise given to Jesus for His finished work of the cross, for, and in all things done by Christ. So as we worship Him, we may offer praise and thanksgiving for His forgiveness of sin as an example. Or for the blessings, we delivered in what we did unto the Lord (1 Corinthians 10:31). So whether to the good works we walked in this life or to the forgiveness of a sin we so committed, we will give Christ praise and blessings.

However, please note that when Jesus comes to judge the world, God will bring none of those sins before we who believe, for Jesus paid for those sins. Therefore, God remembers our sins no more (Hebrews 8:12). But because of now having perfect understandings (Hebrews 12:23) and seeing Jesus constantly before us, our response is praise, adoration, and thanksgiving!

There is a thought out in the Christian world that our eternal life from Heaven forward will be a clean slate; that once in Heaven, God will change more than our bodies. And He will also change what we will remember and our personalities. I don't see that at all. Randy Alcorn, Director of Eternal Perspective Ministries, declares:

> "The idea that we'll lose our identities in heaven is Hindu, not Christian. Resurrection will forever reestablish us as glorified human individuals.
>
> Christ's resurrection is our prototype. He proclaimed, "It is I myself" (Luke 24:39). When Thomas said, "My Lord and my God," he knew he was speaking to the same Jesus he'd lived with for years. Job said, "After my skin has been thus destroyed, yet in my flesh I shall see God, whom I shall see for myself" (Job 19:26–27).
>
> You will be *you* in heaven. Who else would you be? Since we'll give an account of our lives on earth, we must remain us, and our memories will have to be better, not worse. Scripture gives no indication of a memory wipe causing us not to recognize family and friends. In fact, if we wouldn't know our loved ones, the comfort of an afterlife reunion, taught in 1 Thessalonians 4:14–18, would be no comfort at all." **Randy Alcorn Director,**

Eternal Perspective Ministries: https://www.desiringgod. org/articles/let-go-of-lies-about-heaven

Pulled 5/05/22

Rabbit Trail Two: On Earth, In Heaven.

'Our Father who is IN Heaven... ' 'ON Earth as it is IN Heaven. We live on this Earth; does that mean we enter 'INTO' Heaven?

A short answer, Yes.

In Heaven seems to be the correct phrase: There is a whole different 'world' that God created as Heaven - a Spiritual realm where He has His throne. God is everywhere, yet His current dominion is Heaven.

Entrance into Heaven has many aspects.

For one thing, flesh and blood cannot inherit the Kingdom of God - Heaven:

> I tell you this, brothers: flesh and blood cannot inherit the kingdom of God, nor does the perishable inherit the imperishable.

> (1 Corinthians 15:50)

The second thing to note is not everyone can enter.

> Jesus answered him, "Truly, truly, I say to you, unless one is born again he cannot see the kingdom of God."

> Jesus answered, "Truly, truly, I say to you, unless one is born of water and the Spirit, he cannot enter the kingdom of God.

> (John 3:3, 5)

In the plan of God, as believers in Jesus, our citizenship is in Heaven and not on this mortal earth. God creates us through the conception of life - as people born of flesh and blood.

God gifts each of us life at the moment of conception. The Spirit of God sparks our being at the instant of a man's sperm union to a woman's egg.

Life. The miracle of life. Being who Almighty God creates us through actions of humanity. He creates our spirit of who we are and who we become.

From this moment on, the eternal plan for each of us begins to unfold.

> For you formed my inward parts; you knitted me together in my mother's womb. I praise you, for I am fearfully and wonderfully made. Wonderful are your works; my soul knows it very well. My frame was not hidden from you, when I was being made in secret, intricately woven in the depths of the earth. Your eyes saw my unformed substance; in your book were written, every one of them, the days that were formed for me, when as yet there was none of them.

> (Psalms 139:13-16)

Our first birth. The mortal body - given to our soul, God, created for each of us as He had determined through His will before creation began, begins as our spirit of life. At that very instant of conception!

Our second birth. Then to the time God reveals and enables those in Christ as His Spirit shines the Glory of Christ into our hearts through grace by faith. We experience the power of the Holy Spirit 'in our hearts.' As evidenced in reflection on the time we heard the Gospel of Jesus, it made sense. We see the Glory of Jesus, the sinfulness of self, the need for repentance of sin, and the offer of eternal forgiveness – and the grace of God through faith now implanted within us. And then our eternal life happened in our understanding of being Born Again.

Our spiritual body. Now, with the Holy Spirit living within us, He is our surety to life eternal with Christ. When our body dies, our spirit lives on. And with the power of the Holy Spirit, He immediately brings us into the presence of Christ. So now, in our spiritual body - eternal life is realized for a believer in Christ. We are moving from living on Earth in our mortal flesh and sin to a Heavenly body made perfect.

Our Immortal body. Upon Jesus' return to judge the world, all in Christ now receive our new resurrected bodies. Even those who died before birth.

Birth as to birth | Mortal (birth) as to Spiritual (birth)

The physical body yields to the spiritual body.

Our soul (spirit through the Spirit) gives the body life | Our spirit, through the Spirit, fills the resurrected body and gives eternal life.

Our mortal body one day fails, yet our spiritual body lives on.

Finally, our spiritual body joins our new resurrected incorruptible body presented to us by God to live on the new Earth with Jesus in eternal life.

'So one more time, and this time, let's take it from the top.'

As a former musician, it was common at rehearsals for the jazz band leader to say to the band after playing through the first number, 'Okay guys, now this time, play it as you mean it.' 'Ready, set, let's go.'

The Spirit of God created us to be born first to live on this Earth. And we are spiritually made alive in Christ through the Holy Spirit's call of our second birth.

The Spirit of God now lives within us. He has saved us, and He is also sanctifying, teaching, comforting, witnessing, convicting, and testifying to us who Christ is and who we are in Christ, thus conforming us to the image of Christ. So then, at death, this body dies as a seed sheds its outer shell for the inner body, our spiritual body, to emerge.

The Spirit of God transforms our spirit that lives within this mortal body; as Paul called this body, a tent, upon our last breath. God changes our human bodies [tents] into spiritual bodies [buildings].

Then, the resurrection body - now not conceived by parents, but given directly full-grown by God. – is made perfect and without sin to live eternally with Jesus on the new Earth. Once hidden in Christ for a brief time in this old world, our spiritual bodies transition into the eternal abode for life living on the new Earth. Upon Jesus' return to Earth, God will give us our new, resurrected, immortal bodies. Not from man or dust, but now of God through His Spirit!

By application, my wife Sandy was born by the actions of God through His use of her parents. And then she became Born Again through the activities of the Holy Spirit's call to the Gospel in His bestowing upon her God's grace through faith.

On the morning of her death, it only affected her mortal, birthed body, not her eternally-given life in spirit, through the Holy Spirit's call when she was 13 and understood and believed the Gospel of Christ—Born Again.

And as Paul declares, she is now face-to-face with Jesus, shedding her earthly body for her spiritual body. And when the prophecy of Jesus' return to Earth to reign from the world for 1000 years takes place, she and all saints are given our new resurrected, immortal bodies for our spirits to inhabit.

SIDEBAR Three – In Form, Space, and Time.

And also to note, as God is Spirit [John 4:24a] and has no limits in being, is everywhere, and in every space of time. We, who are of His creation, have bounds within our frame, both physically and spiritually. Meaning to say that all of creation has conformity as God has purposed.

> But God gives it a body as he has chosen, and to each kind of seed its own body. For not all flesh is the same, but there is one kind for humans, another for animals, another for birds, and another for fish. There are heavenly bodies and earthly bodies, but the glory of the heavenly is of one kind, and the glory of the earthly is of another. There is one glory of the sun, and another glory of the moon, and another glory of the stars; for star differs from star in glory.
>
> So is it with the resurrection of the dead. What is sown is perishable; what is raised is imperishable. It is sown in dishonor; it is raised in glory. It is sown in weakness; it is raised in power. It is sown a natural body; it is raised a spiritual body. If there is a natural body, there is also a spiritual body.
>
> (1 Corinthians 15:38-44)

So living in our spiritual bodies, we are contained in form, space, and time. Easy translation: God is Spirit, is omniscient, omnipresent - filling in being everywhere at every time - we are and cannot. Our spiritual body still contains us in space and time, as God has purposed in design. So when we are in our spiritual body - it is still a body. And being in our spiritual body is in the pattern of our physical body. For whom God has created us each to be – but is not of flesh and blood.

> I tell you this, brothers: flesh and blood cannot inherit the kingdom of God, nor does the perishable inherit the imperishable.

> (1 Corinthians 15:50)

So know that the saints in Heaven are 'in' their bodies, their spiritual bodies, and live in Christ as Christ lives in them. And although being in spirit, they still have boundaries of space and time. So therefore, knowing that God is everywhere at the same time(s) of every age. The saints and even the angels of Heaven are not. Now:

Will we have or maintain our emotions in Heaven?

The answer is yes. The first observation is complete joy and satisfaction in Christ. I also believe we will retain who we are and remember our lives on earth perfectly. But being joyful and reflecting on a life lived will be redirected, having been made perfect.

As I stated, Jesus will review all our deeds at the judgment. However, through Jesus, all our sins are forgiven and not remembered by God.

> For I will be merciful toward their iniquities, and I will remember their sins no more."

> (Hebrews 8:12)

So when we stand before Jesus, when it is our turn before Him in Judgement, in perfect wisdom, we will remember our earthly past. But God will not mention the sin we did, as He said He would not, but only the goodness He has given us to walk in. So we will remember the times of life on earth. And to the sins we have committed, we will praise Jesus for His forgiveness of all of our sins. Praise God! And in some way, we will always praise Him for saving us from our sins. And that will be, in part, some of our joy.

Letting my imagination run a little. Sandy and maybe our family members with her might be reminiscing about some of the prayer times we had together. Or reflecting upon the times, God answered our prayers for salvation, healing, and Jesus' return?

Thinking out loud here, God cherishes our prayers. So much so that many - if not all of them - He keeps in His 'prayer box.'

> And when he had taken the scroll, the four living creatures and the twenty-four elders fell down before the Lamb, each holding a harp, and golden bowls full of incense, which are the prayers of the saints
>
> (Revelation 5:8)

> And another angel came and stood at the altar with a golden censer, and he was given much incense to offer with the prayers of all the saints on the golden altar before the throne, and the smoke of the incense, with the prayers of the saints, rose before God from the hand of the angel.
>
> (Revelation 8:3-4)

So then, if what I present is correct, some might see a potential conflict within Revelation 21 regarding our not remembering our life on earth. Or do we?

> Then I saw a new heaven and a new earth, for the first heaven and the first earth had passed away, and the sea was no more. And I saw the holy city, new Jerusalem, coming down out of heaven from God, prepared as a bride

adorned for her husband. And I heard a loud voice from the throne saying, **"Behold, the dwelling place of God is with man. He will dwell with them, and they will be his people, and God himself will be with them as their God. He will wipe away every tear from their eyes, and death shall be no more, neither shall there be mourning, nor crying, nor pain anymore, for the former things have passed away."**

(Revelation 21:1-4; emphasis added)

"For behold, I create new heavens and a new earth, and the former things shall not be remembered or come into mind. But be glad and rejoice forever in that which I create; for behold, I create Jerusalem to be a joy, and her people to be a gladness. I will rejoice in Jerusalem and be glad in my people; no more shall be heard in it the sound of weeping and the cry of distress. No more shall there be in it an infant who lives but a few days, or an old man who does not fill out his days, for the young man shall die a hundred years old, and the sinner a hundred years old shall be accursed. They shall build houses and inhabit them; they shall plant vineyards and eat their fruit. They shall not build and another inhabit; they shall not plant and another eat; for like the days of a tree shall the days of my people be, and my chosen shall long enjoy the work of their hands. They shall not labor in vain or bear children for calamity, **for they shall be the offspring of the blessed of the LORD,** and their descendants with them. Before they call I will answer; while they are yet speaking I will hear.

(Isaiah 65:17-24; emphasis added)

Who are the 'their eyes' and the 'they'?
And who are 'His people?

Is this a reference to the Church? Or are these people those who are yet to be created?

This passage of scripture is a fascinating and intricate passage of scripture. At face value, it would say that mourning, crying, and pain is no more. And that all the former things have passed away. I then again ask, who are the 'they'? Once again, I ask, is the reference to the Church? OR, maybe, just maybe, a connection to the time all of Israel is saved? Notice 'for they shall be the offspring.'

So then, does this imply that believers in Christ will one day forget our past? OR does it mean something else? Or do these verses best fit another time and another group of people that God has in view?

I think about what God has planned for the time we are called to live. We who are in Christ will remember the times of our earthly life, for Jesus died for our sins, and we will spend eternity praising Jesus for His sacrificial death through the cross of pain and suffering to His glorious resurrection! So, "their eyes" must point to another group of people in another future time. I see this as a reference to 'saved' Israel.

In Chapter Ten, I begin exploring this in greater detail, so in my understanding of today, we need to know who the audience is. Is it for the saints in Christ or for others in time future?

Our salvation is from sin. Jesus died for our sins. So as you continue to read, remember that Jesus is Lord and Savior for us who believe. That truth will never go away or change. So I am preparing you for my puzzle building of chapters Ten through Fourteen as I explore Revelation 21:1-4 in more detail.

✝ *David R. Rosen* ✝

Can those in Heaven see those of us who remain on Earth?

As I live each day since Sandy's passing, I often reflect on the life stages that Sandy and I enjoyed together. I have now compiled a memory wall in the basement family room of pictures and memorabilia of our life together. Not for us to live in the past. But to celebrate the life God gave us as a family. To be encouraged to the future - being in Christ when we are together again.

On the wall are pictures of the times of our vacations, Christmas and Easter celebrations, our marriage, and our children and grandchildren gracing the family room wall I set aside for myself and my family to remember and enjoy. To pause and reflect. To shed a tear or two to the joy of life turned from the sorrow of absence, that Sandy, Mom, Grammy is no longer here but living life before Jesus!

So that got me thinking. Will those in Heaven also reflect upon those who remain on Earth? Will Sandy think about me as I remember her often, and will she smile as I smile when we do?

My answer is yes. Here is my logic, hopefully rightly dividing the word of God in the process.

Going back to Abraham, Lazarus, and the rich man, Jesus indicated that they all remembered their lives on Earth. And to the point, Abraham knew the life history of both Lazarus and the rich man. So this example shows me that we will retain our memory, and as such, we will have a perfect understanding of remembering our times on this Earth. And that includes people. AND Abraham knew the lives lived of both Lazarus and the rich man. A big hmmm. I wonder?

Jesus tells us that the rich man declared to Abraham that he had five brothers and that they were not 'saved,' for he asked Abraham to send

88

Lazarus back to Earth to warn his brothers about Hades. So they all remembered their time on this Earth.

And as we have learned from their lives on this Earth, they still live. Abraham and Lazarus are now in the Paradise of Heaven. The rich man is in the torment and judgment of Hades. And they all can see each other but can't reach each other.

So this begs my next question. Can the saints in Heaven see current actions of life happening on Earth?

Not sure I have an answer, but let me take a walk at this as I type.

The rich man retained the remembrance of his family, but Jesus did not indicate that he could see his family. So with that, I don't see that as a possibility. Hades is isolated and away from Heaven, and I would also say away from Earth. In Hades, we see there is isolation. The rich man was in anguish and without companions. In Heaven, Abraham and Lazarus are together. And they are in joy.

So now, then, what about those who are in Heaven? Can they, or are they allowed to see life in action on Earth?

Again, Jesus doesn't say that Abraham and Lazarus saw the rich man's brothers. Abraham knew the rich man's brothers would not believe even if Lazarus were able to return to Earth. So for the moment, Jesus doesn't say those in Heaven can see life back on Earth.

HOWEVER. In Matthew 17, the disciples were called to witness and later testify to Jesus' transfiguration - and they also saw Moses and Elijah as they met with Jesus on the mountain.

> And after six days Jesus took with him Peter and James, and John his brother, and led them up a high mountain by themselves. And he was transfigured before them, and

his face shone like the sun, and his clothes became white as light. And behold, there appeared to them Moses and Elijah, talking with him. And Peter said to Jesus, "Lord, it is good that we are here. If you wish, I will make three tents here, one for you and one for Moses and one for Elijah."

(Matthew 17:1-4)

Now, this may be speculation on my part; but Jesus revealed to the disciples His glory as they saw Jesus speaking with Moses and Elijah high upon the mountain. The main focus is the Glory of the Lord, yet Moses and Elijah were also there!

So by inference, I submit that Moses and Elijah had a view of what Jesus was doing on Earth, and they went to meet with Him. So please realize that this thread I'm weaving is fragile, but Moses and Elijah are in Heaven, and now, for this time in history, they have returned to Earth to meet with Jesus as the disciples were witnesses.

Another thin thread of inference to help build my position is:

Therefore, since we are surrounded by so great a cloud of witnesses, let us also lay aside every weight, and sin which clings so closely, and let us run with endurance the race that is set before us, looking to Jesus, the founder and perfecter of our faith, who for the joy that was set before him endured the cross, despising the shame, and is seated at the right hand of the throne of God.

(Hebrews 12:1-2)

"Cloud of witnesses?" In Hebrews 11, the writer gives a great history lesson about the 'Hall of Faith.' For the faith of Abraham, Moses, Abel, Gideon, Barak, Samson, Jephthah, David, and Samuel, and the prophets, the actions of life through faith in God!

And then – then the writer calls them witnesses. BUT collectively, a CLOUD of witnesses.

I hope they can see a view of earthly life to 'watch' the will of God unfold before them.

Let us look once again to Abraham, for Jesus declares:

> Your father Abraham rejoiced that he would see my day.
> He saw it and was glad."

> (John 8:56)

Here the Jews were trying to discredit who Jesus was, even declaring that Jesus was of the devil. But notice that Jesus is telling them that Abraham would one day see Jesus' day on Earth and witness His works. And in that, Jesus says that Abraham indeed saw Jesus' earthly ministries and was glad. Was this when Abraham was alive on Earth, and Jesus gave him a vision of the future? Or, to the day when Abraham entered into Heaven, and he then saw firsthand – being a witness to the day of Jesus' time of life on Earth?

So back to the cloud of witnesses. My heart again - through doing my best to interpret scripture, says that the Saints of Hebrews 11 looked forward to the day of Christ – to the promise. And then, in chapter 12, we read that this cloud of witnesses is now watching - watching us run with endurance the race that is set before us as we also look to Jesus, the founder, and perfecter of our faith.

And then Jesus tells the unbelieving Jews that their 'father' Abraham looked forward to the day of Christ! And he now saw it! And he was GLAD!

So by application, in summary, those in Heaven have a view into Hades, as Abraham and Lazarus had conversations with the rich man. So we see visibility between those in Heaven and those in Hades.

Then Jesus tells the Jews that Abraham will one day see the day of Jesus on Earth. And then Jesus declares that Abraham did see Jesus' day - as Jesus tells the Jews, it is happening before their eyes. And Abraham was glad! And then, all the other saints in Heaven, i.e., the cloud of witnesses, are also watching the actions of the will of God on Earth as they do from Heaven.

So my wife Sandy and all the saints of Heaven have a view back to Earth. Not in any mystical activity. But as a witness to the Glory of Christ, working to the counsel and will of God the Father. And when it is time for Jesus to return to Earth, she and all the saints in Heaven will also witness the events of the seven seals. And when the scroll becomes fully opened, they will follow Jesus to the Earth in meeting in the clouds with those alive in Christ on the Earth and given our new resurrected bodies before the wrath of God commences.

So notice that those in Heaven can see and talk to those in Hades. But Jesus never stated that those in Heaven or Hades could or would speak to those on Earth. So please keep this in mind!

What about our Earthly families now in Heaven with us?

Again, my heart is that our families who precede us into Heaven will have a fond affection in remembrance for each other while on Earth. My further speculation is that all who know each other in Heaven will recall the times of blessings in the Lord on Earth and give Him praise together for the times of life. So again, in my heart of speculation, Lazarus and Abraham are together in Paradise. And they know each other, and they also know the times of life they did.

Conversely, with the rich man as an example, there will be remorse and regret from those in Hades regarding the life they led without Christ, along with torment. So as hard as it may be, those in Heaven will also know those in Hades.

So this got me thinking again. Lazarus knew the rich man. And Lazarus knows that the rich man is in Hades. And thus, Lazarus hears the rich man call out to Abraham about his torment. And Lazarus hears Abraham tell the rich man about his life's story of prosperity. So my conclusion is that both Abraham and Lazarus knew the sins of those in Hades. How did Abraham know unless Abraham now has perfect understanding [Hebrews 12:23]?

We, therefore, will be able to have a view into Hades from Heaven but barred from crossing over into it, for Lazarus and Abraham are in Heaven; the rich man is in great torment in Hades, separated by a great chasm.

Also to note is comfort in Heaven. However, in Hades, there is torment, anguish, and pain.

Every Family in Heaven and on Earth.

For this reason I bow my knees before the Father, **from whom every family in heaven and on earth is named**, that according to the riches of his glory he may grant you to be strengthened with power through his Spirit in your inner being,

(Ephesians 3:14-16; emphasis added)

Family: πατριά

STRONG'S NUMBER:g3965

Dictionary Definition g3965. πατριά patria ; from 3962; lineage, family:--families(1), family(2).

'Every family in Heaven and on Earth is named ... ' makes me pause for a moment. Paul uses this phrase as a field of witness as he prays for the church at Ephesus. Of course, I realize that the main point is a prayer for

God's work in saving those in the church at Ephesus. But it opened the door for me to ponder the question 'every family in heaven' statement as being known in Heaven as bringing a family relationship to Heaven of those God has saved on this Earth.

Will God preserve the relationships of the family known in life - being firstborn in the flesh - now being transformed into the eternal life of immortality through Christ, raised spiritually into Heaven?

I see there is scriptural support for a yes.

So now would be a good time to ask:

Is there Marriage in Heaven? Matthew 22

We will all be 'grown' in that there is no need to procreate, grow, or learn. However, we also saw that there would no longer be teaching and learning in Heaven, for we all would have perfect understanding. So comparing family life on this Earth to Heavenly life is very different from what I imagine it will be.

Having 'many rooms' will probably mean something for our habitat. In slight jest, but really in hope, when my wife died, one of my prayers to God at that moment was my request to have the room next door to Sandy's.

Marriage is not for eternity but is Earthly, mainly for the prospects of generational salvation. Before God created anything, He planned all things, including those in Christ. And through time that God has determined, He makes each believer, He has ordained.

> Let this be recorded for a generation to come, so that a people yet to be created may praise the LORD:

> (Psalms 102:18)

There is no need for procreation in Heaven, so marriage is no longer in Heaven. BUT remembering our marriage between us will still exist, for again Lazarus remembered his past.

My mother and father are now with Jesus, and both will know each other more intimately than on Earth. For sin has been removed for the saints in Heaven. The love they had on this Earth no longer contains a sexual element but is pure and Spiritual, for the Spirit of Christ lives in the redeemed in Heaven. But I would infer their love is no longer possessive towards each other but given in Christ.

And I will also see my mother and father and know them as mom and dad, and yet will also know them as part of the body of Christ.

So I envision the families on Earth who God saves and brings to Himself in Heaven will be known as who they were in this world. But the family relationship will not be the same as it was on Earth. God gives each one a role that He wants of us, as the Twelve Apostles will have their position in the New Jerusalem, as do David and others.

We know we are created by and for Jesus' glory. And that He is the pinnacle of our faith now realized. As families, I will know my earthly father and mother as my father and mother and my wife as my wife, but I don't see us living as a unit in Heaven. Maybe nearby, but not as an earthly household.

And as the Sadducees – who didn't believe in the resurrection – asked Jesus about a man with six brothers who married the same woman after each one died without an heir, asking Jesus as their weak effort to catch Jesus: whose wife is she in the resurrection?"

But Jesus answered them,

"You are wrong, because you know neither the Scriptures nor the power of God. For in the resurrection they neither marry nor are given in marriage, but are like angels in heaven. And as for the resurrection of the dead, have you

not read what was said to you by God: I am the God of
Abraham, and the God of Isaac, and the God of Jacob'?
He is not God of the dead, but of the living."

(Matthew 22:29-32)

Will we know each other? Yes. Will we know and remember our lives
together on this Earth? Yes. Will we still be married in Heaven? No.
Marriage is for this Earth, and the marriage law ends upon death.

> For a married woman is bound by law to her husband
> while he lives, but if her husband dies she is released from
> the law of marriage.

(Romans 7:2)

However, we will remember our marriages as we remember everything
from this life and praise God for the times of our lives in Him.

When God saves a family on Earth and when they die, will the family relationship still be known in Heaven?

I see many examples of generational salvation given by God.

> One who heard us was a woman named Lydia, from
> the city of Thyatira, a seller of purple goods, who was
> a worshiper of God. The Lord opened her heart to pay
> attention to what was said by Paul. And after she was
> baptized, and her household as well, she urged us, saying,
> "If you have judged me to be faithful to the Lord, come to
> my house and stay." And she prevailed upon us.

(Acts 16:14-15)

And the jailer called for lights and rushed in, and trembling with fear he fell down before Paul and Silas. Then he brought them out and said, "Sirs, what must I do to be saved?" And they said, "Believe in the Lord Jesus, and you will be saved, you and your household."

(Acts 16:29-31)

And the LORD your God will circumcise your heart and the heart of your offspring, so that you will love the LORD your God with all your heart and with all your soul, that you may live.

(Deuteronomy 30:6)

So we see that God can save families when according to the gracious intentions of His will. And in His grace, He reveals and enables in His work of salvation in us so that we know Him, love Him, and worship and live for Him. So I see God can purpose this in the eternal that our life in Him individually and then in relationship to those He also calls from within our household that follows us into Heaven.

When David sinned by raping Bathsheba and then killing her husband, Nathan confronts David with David's sin of rape and murder.

David said to Nathan, "I have sinned against the LORD." And Nathan said to David, "The LORD also has put away your sin; you shall not die. Nevertheless, because by this deed you have utterly scorned the LORD, the child who is born to you shall die." Then Nathan went to his house.

(2 Samuel 12:13-15)

And now, seeing his sin before him, David sought God. David pleaded with God to preserve the life of his son that he fathered with Bathsheba. But as God declared His righteous judgment, the child became sick and died. I say all this to show that God will save families when it is according to His will. First, David repented for the sins he committed against God. Then David accepted the discipline of God for his sin. David also knew of God's grace in the end that he would see his son alive again! But not in the healing of the child's illness, but through the eternal gift of salvation for the child, David knew of God's grace, love, and mercy in salvation.

> But now he is dead. Why should I fast? Can I bring him back again? I shall go to him, but he will not return to me."

> (2 Samuel 12:23)

In David's heart about his sin, he penned Psalms 51, for which I quote an excerpt.

> Have mercy on me, O God, according to your steadfast love; according to your abundant mercy blot out my transgressions. Wash me thoroughly from my iniquity, and cleanse me from my sin! For I know my transgressions, and my sin is ever before me. Against you, you only, have I sinned and done what is evil in your sight, so that you may be justified in your words and blameless in your judgment.

> Create in me a clean heart, O God, and renew a right spirit within me. Cast me not away from your presence, and take not your Holy Spirit from me. Restore to me the joy of your salvation, and uphold me with a willing spirit.

> (Psalms 51:1-4;10-12)

There is much more to gleam from David's snippet of life, his sins, and God's righteousness - but for the point of family in Heaven, even in David's confession of sin towards God, David knew that he would see his son again. AND that his son is before God. My one takeaway is in God's salvation towards us. God maintains family relationships in Heaven, but not as it was on Earth. For all the saints in Heaven are made perfect.

> And *to the assembly of the firstborn who are enrolled in heaven,* and *to God, the judge of all,* and **to the spirits of the righteous made perfect,** and *to Jesus, the mediator of a new covenant,* and *to the sprinkled blood that speaks a better word than the blood of Abel.*

> (Hebrews 12:23-24; emphasis added)

Although we know this world is sinful, we also know that Jesus paid the price for that curse for those who believe He is The Christ, our Savior.

With our last breath, God gives us Christ's perfection. Our old sinful body is no more. Our new spiritual body brings a perfect understanding of sin and the obedience of Christ now known, and we will live with Him in praise and adoration for our salvation.

Taking a closer look at Hebrews 12:23-24.

To the assembly of the firstborn – those of us who believe. Whose names are also written in the Book of Life, i.e., those who are enrolled in heaven. And to God, the judge of all men. And to those who have died in Christ, the spirits of the righteous, and are now called saints – are made perfect by God.

And to Jesus, who is our mediator of the New Covenant, through His shed blood on the Cross of Pain and Suffering, that speaks a better word than the blood of Abel, whose blood was first shed - through sin, and not for sin's eradication, as Jesus' death accomplished.

I say all that to say that we will perfectly know all the saints in Heaven. Because God changes our hearts to believe in the Glory of Jesus here in this life [John 3:5-6; 2 Corinthians 4:6], He will also make us perfect before Himself [through Himself] when He gives us our spiritual bodies for Heaven.

Learning will stop, and we will gain perfect understanding. Now our sinning is finished, and through the perfection, God has given us in our heavenly bodies, we are made clean by Jesus' finished work of the cross, realized before Him in Heaven!

In Heaven will each day be remembered?

On Earth, each day has opportunities for events to be retained within our minds – memories. But will we also remember each day in Heaven?

I believe so. Having been made perfect, I would ascribe that would also include having perfect understanding and indicate having our remembrances of life retained. As created beings of God, He has given us the ability to think, plan, and do life here on this Earth, yet our lives here are in and with sin. But in Heaven, sin is eradicated for the saints through the blood and finished work of Jesus, so living now in the perfection of Christ, I highly suspect we will also remember each moment of Glory we will experience and be satisfied immensely.

As stated above, Abraham witnessed the day of Jesus, and I believe He did so from Heaven. And Jesus declared that Abraham was glad! So again, my heart would say that Abraham will continue to offer his praise before Jesus for Jesus' fulfilling the will of the Father as each day unfolds!

So our lives, our hearts, and our actions will be made perfect, and our minds will be in sinless perfection. And as we will remember life on Earth by praising Jesus, our efforts in eternity will also be perfect and remembered with praise and adoration of Christ.

Who are the Occupants of Heaven?

Reflecting on my earlier observations about Heaven as a place, and for the lack of a better term that I can think of, another dimension, maybe it's time to reintroduce and summarize who all live there.

We know that God the Father and Jesus reside there. We also know that angels do as well. And we also have a glimpse into who is in attendance within the throne room of God.

The Seraphim:

> Above him stood the seraphim. Each had six wings: with two he covered his face, and with two he covered his feet, and with two he flew.

> (Isaiah 6:2)

The Four Living Creatures:

> And from the midst of it came the likeness of four living creatures. And this was their appearance: they had a human likeness, but each had four faces, and each of them had four wings. Their legs were straight, and the soles of their feet were like the sole of a calf's foot. And they sparkled like burnished bronze. Under their wings on their four sides they had human hands. And the four had their faces and their wings thus: their wings touched one another. Each one of them went straight forward, without turning as they went. As for the likeness of their faces, each had a human face. The four had the face of a lion on the right side, the four had the face of an ox on the left side, and the four had the face of an eagle. Such were their faces. And their wings were spread out above. Each creature had two wings, each of which touched the

wing of another, while two covered their bodies. And each went straight forward. Wherever the spirit would go, they went, without turning as they went. As for the likeness of the living creatures, their appearance was like burning coals of fire, like the appearance of torches moving to and fro among the living creatures. And the fire was bright, and out of the fire went forth lightning. And the living creatures darted to and fro, like the appearance of a flash of lightning.

(Ezekiel 1:5-14)

And around the throne, on each side of the throne, are four living creatures, full of eyes in front and behind: the first living creature like a lion, the second living creature like an ox, the third living creature with the face of a man, and the fourth living creature like an eagle in flight. And the four living creatures, each of them with six wings, are full of eyes all around and within, and day and night they never cease to say, "Holy, holy, holy, is the Lord God Almighty, who was and is and is to come!"

(Revelation 4:6-8)

The Twenty-four Elders:

Around the throne were twenty-four thrones, and seated on the thrones were twenty-four elders, clothed in white garments, with golden crowns on their heads.

(Revelation 4:4)

Angels:

The chariots of God are twenty thousand, even thousands of angels.

(Psalms 68:17a)

For he shall give his angels charge over thee, to keep thee in all thy ways.

(Psalms 91:11)

The Son of man shall send forth his angels, and they shall gather out of his kingdom all things that offend, and them which do iniquity.

(Matthew 13:41)

And in the sixth month the angel Gabriel was sent from God unto a city of Galilee, named Nazareth.

(Luke 1:26)

Archangels:

[9] But when the archangel Michael, contending with the devil, was disputing about the body of Moses, he did not presume to pronounce a blasphemous judgment, but said, "The Lord rebuke you."

(Jude 1:9)

The Saints now in heaven:

> In my Father's house are many rooms. If it were not so, would I have told you that I go to prepare a place for you?
>
> (John 14:2)

Satan and his angels:

> Now war arose in heaven, Michael and his angels fighting against the dragon. And the dragon and his angels fought back, but he was defeated, and there was no longer any place for them in heaven.
>
> (Revelation 12:7-8)

So as with Earth, God has created all kinds of life for Heaven and Earth. And each being God has created has a role and a function for the Glory of God. So we will see people, angels, beings, and elders, along with Jesus. And I highly suspect we will see the glory of God the Father, as one day the Glory of God the Father and the Son will be the light of the New World.

> And I saw no temple in the city, for its temple is the Lord God the Almighty and the Lamb. And the city has no need of sun or moon to shine on it, for the glory of God gives it light, and its lamp is the Lamb.
>
> (Revelation 21:22-23)

CHAPTER 8

First Fruits, Rapture, Resurrection.

Are these different words for the same event? Or are these succinct events? Or both?

Let us explore.

The first observation I have is that they all deal with a transformation. And I would also note that the rapture and the resurrection all reference our physical bodies.

First Fruits

> But in fact Christ has been raised from the dead, the firstfruits of those who have fallen asleep. For as by a man came death, by a man has come also the resurrection of the dead. For as in Adam all die, so also in Christ shall all be made alive. But each in his own order: Christ the firstfruits, then at his coming those who belong to Christ. Then comes the end, when he delivers the kingdom to God the Father after destroying every rule and every authority and power. For he must reign until he has put all his enemies under his feet. The last enemy to be destroyed is death.
>
> (1 Corinthians 15:20-26)

Although Jesus is not the first man to die, he is the first man to be resurrected into eternal, immortal life. Therefore, because He lives, all believers will live again in the resurrection.

> And not only the creation, but we ourselves, who have the firstfruits of the Spirit, groan inwardly as we wait eagerly for adoption as sons, the redemption of our bodies.
>
> (Romans 8:23)

Because of Christ's finished work of the cross, and because in faith, we are born again, and in His Spirit, we will live in our bodies - our new resurrected eternal bodies - again!

Sandy, and to all the saints in Heaven and on Earth today - are the first fruits of the resurrection.

> But we ought always to give thanks to God for you, brothers beloved by the Lord, because God chose you as the firstfruits to be saved, through sanctification by the Spirit and belief in the truth.
>
> (2 Thessalonians 2:13)

> Of his own will he brought us forth by the word of truth, that we should be a kind of firstfruits of his creatures.
>
> (James 1:18)

Historical to my studies, when I came to scripture speaking of first fruits, I usually read past this to focus on the other words of context, not going deeper into the understanding. But with my wife's passing, I'm taking a slower and more diligent read about Heaven than before and asking God to help me to understand the first fruits better.

The first fruit is an agricultural term. It indicates the farming results when [good] seeds are planted into the cultivated soil at the beginning of the growing season. And then, through the attention of water, sun, and time, fruit starts to appear.

Growth for the whole crop doesn't happen all at once. It's like the business bell curve. Some plants will produce first; then, the majority will arrive for harvesting in a little while. And lastly, a few plants are the laggards.

We couldn't wait for the season's first corn to arrive at our house. The first meal with corn on the cob was always welcomed with delicious anticipation, being tasty, sweet, and better than what was frozen or canned.

From there, we knew that more corn would be ready and be on its way in the months ahead, for the first fruit was our sign that the harvest was near.

Jesus is the first fruit of the Resurrection. Because of His finished work of the cross, He is the first of the first. [Having His physical, immortal, resurrected body.]

The Apostle Paul tells us through his letters that we are within the Firstfruits of the Resurrection. So then, at Jesus' coming, those who are dead in Christ, with those who are alive in Christ - are also the first fruits of the Resurrection. As Paul declares: "For as in Adam all die, so also in Christ shall all be made alive. But each in his own order: Christ the first fruits, then at his coming those who belong to Christ."

> But each in his own order: Christ the firstfruits, then at his coming those who belong to Christ. Then comes the end, when he delivers the kingdom to God the Father after destroying every rule and every authority and power. For he must reign until he has put all his enemies under his feet. The last enemy to be destroyed is death. For "God has put all things in subjection under his feet." But when it says, "all things are put in subjection," it is plain that

he is excepted who put all things in subjection under him. When all things are subjected to him, then the Son himself will also be subjected to him who put all things in subjection under him, that God may be all in all.

(1 Corinthians 15:23-28)

I built a small table to help see the cause and effect of the resurrection that Paul is declaring about dying to live.

1 Corinthians 15:42-45
So is it with the resurrection of the dead.

What is sown is perishable	What is raised is imperishable
It is sown in dishonor	It is raised in glory
It is sown in weakness	It is raised in power
It is sown a natural body	It is raised a spiritual body
If there is a natural body	There is also a spiritual body

Thus it is written,

"The first man Adam became a living being"	The last Adam became a life-giving spirit.

But in fact Christ has been raised from the dead, the firstfruits of those who have fallen asleep. For as by a man came death, by a man has come also the resurrection of the dead. For as in Adam all die, so also in Christ shall all be made alive. But each in his own order: Christ the firstfruits, then at his coming those who belong to Christ. Then comes the end, when he delivers the kingdom to God the Father after destroying every rule and every authority and power. For he must reign until he has put all his enemies under his feet. The last enemy to be destroyed is death.

(1 Corinthians 15:20-26)

1. Christ the First fruit
2. At His coming – those who belong to Christ – are part of the first fruits.
3. Then the end comes – when Jesus delivers the kingdom to God the Father –
4. After destroying those in rule, power, and sin.
5. Prior to handing the kingdom back to God, Jesus must reign until He puts all his enemies under His feet.
6. With the last enemy to be destroyed is death.

SIDEBAR Four – Seeds.

What happens to a seed?

Seeds have outer shells covering the softer inner parts of the seed of a plant. A seed is placed into the soil [sown], and the seed loses its outer shell as the internal, more delicate parts push it away to take on the nutrients of the ground and the water to develop [raised].

The shell of the seed is pushed away by the inner matter to reproduce into a newer "body," i.e., mortal – Spiritual- immortal.

So we are born into corruption. We are reborn by the Holy Spirit into salvation. In, by, and through Jesus, who now lives within us - as the inner part of the seed. And when our mortal bodies die, our spiritual bodies overtake the former shell of our mortal bodies. Then, when Jesus returns at the Rapture, our new immortal, imperishable bodies are given to us, and the seeds maturation is complete.

Rapture.

For since we believe that Jesus died and rose again, even so, through Jesus, God will bring with him those who have fallen asleep [died]. For this we declare to you by a word from the Lord, that we who are alive, who are left until the coming of the Lord, will not precede those who have fallen asleep. For the Lord himself will descend from heaven with a cry of command, with the voice of an archangel, and with the sound of the trumpet of God. And the dead in Christ will rise first. Then we who are alive, who are left, will be caught up together with them in the clouds to meet the Lord in the air, and so we will always be with the Lord. Therefore encourage one another with these words.

(1 Thessalonians 4:14-18)

I tell you this, brothers: flesh and blood cannot inherit the kingdom of God, nor does the perishable inherit the imperishable. Behold! I tell you a mystery. We shall not all sleep, but we shall all be changed, in a moment, in the twinkling of an eye, at the last trumpet. For the trumpet will sound, and the dead will be raised imperishable, and we shall be changed. For this perishable body must put on the imperishable, and this mortal body must put on immortality. When the perishable puts on the imperishable, and the mortal puts on immortality, then shall come to pass the saying that is written:

"Death is swallowed up in victory." "O death, where is your victory? O death, where is your sting?" The sting of death is sin, and the power of sin is the law. But thanks be to God, who gives us the victory through our Lord Jesus Christ.

(1 Corinthians 15:50-57)

This is evidence of the righteous judgment of God, that you may be considered worthy of the kingdom of God, for which you are also suffering— since indeed God considers it just to repay with affliction those who afflict you, and to grant relief to you who are afflicted as well as to us, when the Lord Jesus is revealed from heaven with his mighty angels in flaming fire, inflicting vengeance on those who do not know God and on those who do not obey the gospel of our Lord Jesus. They will suffer the punishment of eternal destruction, away from the presence of the Lord and from the glory of his might, when he comes on that day to be glorified in his saints, and to be marveled at among all who have believed, because our testimony to you was believed. To this end we always pray for you, that our God may make you worthy of his calling and may fulfill every resolve for good and every work of faith by his power, so that the name of our Lord Jesus may be glorified in you, and you in him, according to the grace of our God and the Lord Jesus Christ.

Now concerning the coming of our Lord Jesus Christ and our being gathered together to him, we ask you, brothers, not to be quickly shaken in mind or alarmed, either by a spirit or a spoken word, or a letter seeming to be from us, to the effect that the day of the Lord has come. Let no one deceive you in any way. For that day will not come, unless the rebellion comes first, and the man of lawlessness is revealed, the son of destruction, who opposes and exalts himself against every so-called god or object of worship, so that he takes his seat in the temple of God, proclaiming

himself to be God. Do you not remember that when I
was still with you I told you these things? And you know
what is restraining him now so that he may be revealed
in his time.

(2 Thessalonians 2:1-12)

For you have died, and your life is hidden with Christ in
God. When Christ who is your life appears, then you also
will appear with him in glory.

(Colossians 3:3-4)

As a reminder - I'm looking at the Rapture through the eyes of my wife,
Sandy, who is with Jesus in Heaven; her next stage of life happens when
Jesus is sent by God the Father back to the Earth.

And then they will see the Son of Man coming in clouds
with great power and glory. And then he will send out the
angels and gather his elect from the four winds, from the
ends of the earth to the ends of heaven.

(Mark 13:26-27)

Scholarly postulating and positioning happens within Christendom
during the rapture and resurrection timings. Are they different names
for the same event? Or are they two separate events that bring the same
results? And does Jesus return twice, once for the Rapture and the next
for His judgment?

Of course, we all know and understand that Scripture declares that the
Rapture brings our resurrected bodies. But my question is then, once
we are all in the air with Christ in the rapture/resurrection, where does
Scripture say we all go next?

Some in academic circles say we go back to Heaven. Other scholars say we then go to Earth. Even others say this is our wedding time.

Before I continue, I want to declare the utmost respect for the men and women of faith that I am about to quote in disagreement. These men are Bible-trained, college-trained, and hold many degrees from their studies. And most are teachers to teachers. Therefore, by education alone, I am outclassed.

And they have solid ministries, too, and I even have 'gone to school' within their media ministries in gleaming insight into other biblical topics of my study.

But with all due respect, I have learned to test all things, hold on to the good [1 Thessalonian 5:21], and in that, I need to justify to myself what I can defend in understanding, as the Holy Spirit reveals to my heart.

It is not my intent to discredit these men but to shine the light of the sum of thy Word of truth that I understand and can defend.

So with that as a backdrop, here is where Dr. David Jeremiah takes the position that Jesus returns twice.

Pretribulation as Told by Dr. David Jeremiah.

"What Is the Difference Between the Rapture and the Second Coming?

https://www.davidjeremiah.org/age-of-signs/what-is-the-difference-between-the-rapture-and-the-second-coming Pulled 5/22/22

This is one of prophecy's greatest misconceptions. The Rapture and the Second Coming are often confused, but they are distinct events, with distinct purposes, on God's prophetic timeline.

At the Rapture, Jesus will return *for* His saints. At the Second Coming, He will return *with* His saints.

At the Rapture, Jesus will not descend to earth. At the Second Coming, He will descend to the Mount of Olives as a prelude to His earthly reign.

At the Rapture, Jesus will bring a blessing for His saints. At the Second Coming, He will bring judgment for those who have rejected Him.

The Rapture could occur at any moment. The Second Coming will occur seven years later.

When the Rapture occurs, Christ will take every deceased and every living Christian to heaven with Him. Paul describes this glorious event in 1 Thessalonians 4:16–17:

For the Lord Himself will descend from heaven with a shout, with the voice of an archangel, and with the trumpet of God. And the dead in Christ will rise first. Then we who are alive and remain shall be caught up together with them in the clouds to meet the Lord in the air. And thus we shall always be with the Lord.

The Rapture will protect God's saints from the Tribulation—the seven years of judgment that will be poured out on earth between the Rapture and the Second Coming. There are some who argue the Tribulation period will begin before the Rapture. However, the Bible says that "there is therefore now no condemnation to those who are in Christ Jesus" (Romans 8:1), which suggests the Church will not experience God's judgment during the Tribulation.

Seven years after the Rapture, Jesus will return to earth
in the event known as the Second Coming. His return
will be entirely different from His arrival in Bethlehem
as a humble Child. When Christ returns, He will appear
as the exalted King of the universe, surrounded by His
saints. The powers of evil will be quickly defeated at the
Battle of Armageddon, and then Christ will establish His
everlasting kingdom on earth.

For a more thorough study of the Rapture and the Second
Coming, read chapters 12 and 27 in *The Book of Signs*."

First, I am concerned with his first statement that Jesus returns twice, once
in the air and the second time to the ground. And in that, those in Heaven
return to Heaven? And those on Earth will have their newly resurrected
bodies in Heaven and not on Earth? I see scripture through Jesus' words
of Matthew 24, connecting them as one event.

"Immediately after the tribulation of those days the sun
will be darkened, and the moon will not give its light,
and the stars will fall from heaven, and the powers of the
heavens will be shaken. **Then** will appear in heaven the
sign of the Son of Man, **and then all the tribes of the earth
will mourn**, and they will see the Son of Man coming on
the clouds of heaven with power and great glory. And he
will send out his angels with a loud trumpet call, **and they
will gather his elect** from the four winds, from one end of
heaven to the other.

(Matthew 24:29-31)

Dr. Jeremiah presents two returns of Jesus. He states – "This is one of the
prophecy's greatest misconceptions. The Rapture and the Second Coming
are often confused, but they are distinct events, with distinct purposes, on

God's prophetic timeline. At the Rapture, Jesus will return for His saints. At the Second Coming, He will return with His saints."

Please take note that Jesus declares that everyone on Earth will see Jesus coming. And, those in Christ will rise to be with Him. And all the rest on Earth who are not in Christ will mourn, and even hide when they see Him coming:

> When he opened the sixth seal, I looked, and behold, there was a great earthquake, and the sun became black as sackcloth, the full moon became like blood, and the stars of the sky fell to the earth as the fig tree sheds its winter fruit when shaken by a gale. The sky vanished like a scroll that is being rolled up, and every mountain and island was removed from its place. **Then** the kings of the earth and the great ones and the generals and the rich and the powerful, and everyone, slave and free, hid themselves in the caves and among the rocks of the mountains, calling to the mountains and rocks, "Fall on us and hide us from the face of him who is seated on the throne, and from **the wrath of the Lamb, for the great day of their wrath has come, and who can stand?"**
>
> (Revelation 6:12-17)

Dr. Jeremiah then states that we go back to Heaven with Jesus:

> "When the Rapture occurs, Christ will take every deceased and every living Christian to heaven with Him. Paul describes this glorious event in 1 Thessalonians 4:16–17:
>
> *For the Lord Himself will descend from heaven with a shout, with the voice of an archangel, and with the trumpet of God. And the dead in Christ will rise first. Then we who*

are alive and remain shall be caught up together with them
in the clouds to meet the Lord in the air. And thus we shall
always be with the Lord." Ibid.

Are we returning to heaven? I cannot see this as so. Paul writes that we will always be with the Lord. And respectfully, are not those who have died before Jesus' return for them - already in Heaven with Jesus? Paul declares in 2 Corinthians 5:8, 'Absent from the body, present [at home] with the Lord.' Will heaven, where the saints in heaven are currently with Jesus, will they leave heaven to return quickly? And will heaven hold our immortal physical bodies for a season? [For flesh and blood cannot inherit the kingdom of [in] heaven [1 Corinthians 15:50]]

With God, nothing is impossible; but does He tell us that this will happen? I don't see it as so.

And I disagree with his position that scripture calls all seven years - thus implying the opening of the seven seals to the scroll - are of God's judgments on the world.

Dr. Jerimiah continues:

"The Rapture will protect God's saints from the Tribulation—the seven years of judgment that will be poured out on earth between the Rapture and the Second Coming. There are some who argue the Tribulation period will begin before the Rapture. However, the Bible says that "there is therefore now no condemnation to those who are in Christ Jesus" (Romans 8:1), which suggests the Church will not experience God's judgment during the Tribulation.

Seven years after the Rapture, Jesus will return to earth in the event known as the Second Coming. His return will be entirely different from His arrival in Bethlehem as a humble Child. When Christ returns, He will appear as the exalted King of the universe, surrounded by His saints. The powers of evil will be quickly defeated at the Battle of Armageddon, and then Christ will establish His everlasting kingdom on earth" ibid..

Dr. Jeremiah thus holds a Pretribulation Rapture position within his statement. And, per Gotquestions.org, I have grabbed their definition of pretribulation for us to understand.

> "Pretribulationism teaches that the Rapture occurs before the Tribulation starts. At that time, the church will meet Christ in the air, and then sometime after that the Antichrist is revealed and the Tribulation begins. In other words, the Rapture and Christ's Second Coming (to set up His kingdom) are separated by at least seven years. According to this view, the church does not experience any of the Tribulation."

> [Gotquestions.Org https://www.gotquestions.org/ pretribulationism.html Pulled 05/22/22]

Note that the Pretribulation position believes that it ties the actions of Revelation 6 and the opening of the seven seals to the wrath of God.

As I have shared within my second book, En Route to the Mount of Olives – Matthew 24, the opening of the first five seals releases the wrath of Satan, culminating when the fifth seal is opened:

> When he opened the fifth seal, I saw under the altar the souls of those who had been slain for the word of God and for the witness they had borne. They cried out with a loud voice, "O Sovereign Lord, holy and true, how long before you will judge and avenge our blood on those who dwell on the earth?" Then they were each given a white robe and

told to rest a little longer, until the number of their fellow servants and their brothers should be complete, who were to be killed as they themselves had been.

(Revelation 6:9-11)

If the fifth seal is part of God's wrath, why would God slay those who are a witness for Jesus, and are now under the altar, having died [killed] for their faith in Jesus during the Great Tribulation? If the opening of the seven seals brings forward the wrath of God, as Dr. Jeremiah declares, why do people die for their faith in Jesus if this is the Wrath of God?

So for your further consideration, what if the seals are stages to the wrath of Satan and the antichrist?

Now war arose in heaven, Michael and his angels fighting against the dragon. And the dragon and his angels fought back, but he was defeated, and there was no longer any place for them in heaven. And the great dragon was thrown down, that ancient serpent, who is called the devil and Satan, the deceiver of the whole world—he was thrown down to the earth, and his angels were thrown down with him.

Therefore, rejoice, O heavens and you who dwell in them! But woe to you, O earth and sea, for the devil has come down to you in great wrath, because he knows that his time is short!"

(Revelation 12:7-9, 12)

So let us go back to the Rapture and Resurrection. Are they the same? I would say yes. When the rapture occurs, Jesus returns, as Matthew 24 declares, and the saints meet Jesus in the air. And we will be given our immortal, resurrected bodies and be with Jesus.

The Moody Bible Institute.

Supposing my challenge to Dr. David Jeremiah's eschatology disrupts the pretribulation viewpoint for his followers. Then my critique of the similar position of the Moody Bible Institute will also undoubtedly be challenging for some to see. Therefore, I pray that we let scripture - through the instruction of the Holy Spirit - challenge our thinking and not just my words.

https://www.moodybible.org/beliefs/positional-statements/second-coming/ Pulled 5/22/22

The Second Coming of Christ

We believe in the second coming of Christ. His return from heaven will be personal, visible and glorious, a blessed hope for which we should constantly watch and pray.[1]

Before He establishes His kingdom on earth, Jesus will come for His Church, an event commonly referred to as the "Rapture." At that time the dead in Christ will be raised and living Christians will be caught up to meet the Lord in the air and be with Him forever.[2] In this resurrection, those who have died in Christ will have their redeemed souls and spirits united with a body similar to Christ's glorified body. Christians living at the time of this event will not die, but will be changed to be like Christ.[3] This expectation is a motivation for holy living, as well as a source of comfort.[4] No man knows the day or the hour when this will take place.[5]"

[So far, so good; for I agree with the above, except for the word "Church." I understand that all the Old Testament saints who looked to the promise of Jesus' salvation will also receive their new resurrected bodies and share in the first fruits of the resurrection.]

"After the Rapture of the Church, Christians will be brought before the judgment seat of Christ. He will reward them on the basis of the works they have accomplished.[6] This is not a judgment to determine their salvation but a reward for labor on Christ's behalf.[7] The Rapture will also inaugurate a period that the Bible characterizes as the "great day of His wrath," "the great tribulation" and the "time of Jacob's trouble."[8]"

[So I agree with everything stated in the phrase "great day of His wrath." But from there, I again disagree that God's wrath is the Great Tribulation. The Great Tribulation is the wrath of Satan – See Revelation 12:12 quoted above.]

"This time of unprecedented difficulty will affect Israel and all nations. Its purpose will be to prepare Israel for her Messiah.[9]"

[My question concerns God sealing the 144,000. These folks will become saved Israel, and God will protect them from both Satan and God's wrath. Let us look for the 144,000 and see who they are, where they are, and what happens to them compared with Moody's position]

After this I saw four angels standing at the four corners of the earth, holding back the four winds of the earth, that no wind might blow on earth or sea or against any tree. Then I saw another angel ascending from the rising of the sun, with the seal of the living God, and **he called with a loud voice** to the four angels who had been given power to harm earth and sea, saying, "Do not harm the earth or the sea or the trees, until **we** have sealed the servants of our God on their foreheads." And I heard the number of

the sealed, 144,000, sealed from every tribe of the sons
of Israel:

12,000 from the tribe of Judah were sealed,
12,000 from the tribe of Reuben,
12,000 from the tribe of Gad,
12,000 from the tribe of Asher,
12,000 from the tribe of Naphtali,
12,000 from the tribe of Manasseh,
12,000 from the tribe of Simeon,
12,000 from the tribe of Levi,
12,000 from the tribe of Issachar,
12,000 from the tribe of Zebulun,
12,000 from the tribe of Joseph,
12,000 from the tribe of Benjamin were sealed.

(Revelation 7:1-8; emphasis added)

Then I looked, and behold, **on Mount Zion stood the
Lamb,** and with him 144,000 who had his name and his
Father's name written on their foreheads. And I heard a
voice from heaven like the roar of many waters and like
the sound of loud thunder. The voice I heard was like the
sound of harpists playing on their harps, and they were
singing a new song before the throne and before the four
living creatures and before the elders. No one could learn
that song except the 144,000 who had been redeemed
from the earth. It is these who have not defiled themselves
with women, for they are virgins. It is these who follow the
Lamb wherever he goes. These have been redeemed from
mankind as firstfruits for God and the Lamb, and in their
mouth no lie was found, for they are blameless.

(Revelation 14:1-5)

[So another question that Moody implies but without accounting for the 144,000.]

"At the end of the Tribulation, Jesus Christ will return with the hosts of heaven as well as the Church to establish the Messianic Kingdom on earth."

[As with Dr. Jeremiah, Moody also declares two returns of Jesus.]

"[10] His Kingdom will last for a thousand years.[11] At this Second Coming, the Antichrist will be cast into the Lake of Fire and Satan will be bound for a thousand years." [ibid]

['At this Second Coming … ' Do they mean Jesus' second coming or a second, second coming?]

""[12] The nations and their representatives will be judged.[13] Israel will be restored to her land, never more to be removed.[14] Christ will reign with firmness and equity.[15] His kingdom will be marked by material and spiritual blessing, since the curse upon the earth will be removed.[16]"

[' … The curse upon the earth will be removed,' during the millennial kingdom - is not what I see what the bible declares. Sin will still be possible, and in Revelation 21, with the new heaven and earth – then is the time sin and corruption will be no more"]

"The Messianic kingdom will close with apostasy and rebellion.[17] God will crush this uprising in the last battle of the ages and Satan will be thrown into the lake of fire.[18] All those who rejected the Word of God will be resurrected.[19] They will be judged by Christ and cast into the lake of fire, the place where they will suffer final and everlasting punishment.[20]

After this judgment there will be a new heaven and a new earth, where righteousness is the norm.[21] There will be a new Jerusalem and the everlasting presence of God among all the redeemed.[22]"

[1] Zechariah 14:4; Acts 1:11; Titus 2:13; Revelation 1:7
[2] 1 Corinthians 15:51–54; 1 Thessalonians 4:14
[3] 1 John 3:2
[4] 1 John 2:28; 1 Thessalonians 4:18
[5] Matt. 24:36; John 6:39
[6] Romans 14:10–12; 2 Corinthians 5:10
[7] 1 Corinthians 3:9–15
[8] Revelation 6:17; 7:14; Jeremiah 30:7
[9] Zechariah 12:2, 3; 14:1–3
[10] Revelation 19:7–9, 14; 1 Thessalonians 3:13; Zechariah 14:9; Revelation 19:15, 16
[11] Revelation 20:2, 4–6
[12] Revelation 19:20; 20:1–3
[13] Joel 3; Matthew 25
[14] Amos 9:15; Ezekiel 34:28
[15] Psalms 2:9; Isaiah 11:4
[16] Romans 8:19-21
[17] Revelation 20:7–9
[18] Revelation 20:10
[19] Revelation 20:11–13
[20] Revelation 20:14, 15; Mark 9:48
[21] 2 Peter 3:13
[22] Revelation 21:2, 3; 2:3–5"

END MOODY BIBLE INSTITUTE QUOTE.

So you may be asking, why is this important? The first reason is that it's the word of God!

'I love those who love me, and those who seek me diligently find me."

(Proverbs 8:17)

Another reason is for the Joy of Jesus!, To know the fullness of His glory as He gives us insight through His word!

And down the line of the whys lies knowing the experience of life after death. Using my wife again as our guide, she lives with Jesus in Heaven today. And she is in community with all the saints of Heaven, waiting for God to send Jesus back to Earth. If Jesus comes in my lifetime, I will join with her and all the saints from Heaven to meet Jesus in the air, and He will bestow our new resurrected immortal bodies. And for us alive on earth, we will always be with Jesus, just as my wife is now.

Resurrection.

> But someone will ask, "How are the dead raised? With what kind of body do they come?" You foolish person! What you sow does not come to life unless it dies. And what you sow is not the body that is to be, but a bare kernel, perhaps of wheat or of some other grain. But God gives it a body as he has chosen, and to each kind of seed its own body.
>
> (1 Corinthians 15:35-38)

So is it with the resurrection of the dead. What is sown is perishable; what is raised is imperishable. It is sown in dishonor; it is raised in glory. It is sown in weakness; it is raised in power. It is sown a natural body; it is raised a spiritual body. If there is a natural body, there is also a spiritual body. Thus it is written, "The first man Adam became a living being;" the last Adam became a life-giving spirit. But it is not the spiritual that is first but the natural, and then the spiritual. The first man was from the earth, a man of dust; the second man is from heaven. As was the man of dust, so also are those who are of the dust, and as is the man of heaven, so also are those who are of heaven. Just as we have borne the image of the man of dust, we shall also bear the image of the man of heaven.

(1 Corinthians 15:42-49)

For we know that if the tent that is our earthly home is destroyed, we have a building from God, a house not made with hands, eternal in the heavens. For in this tent we groan, longing to put on our heavenly dwelling, if indeed by putting it on we may not be found naked. For while we are still in this tent, we groan, being burdened— not that we would be unclothed, but that we would be further clothed, so that what is mortal may be swallowed up by life. He who has prepared us for this very thing is God, who has given us the Spirit as a guarantee.

So we are always of good courage. We know that while we are at home in the body we are away from the Lord, for we walk by faith, not by sight. Yes, we are of good courage, and we would rather be away from the body and at home with the Lord.

(2 Corinthians 5:1-8)

For in the resurrection they neither marry nor are given in marriage, but are like angels in heaven. And as for the resurrection of the dead, have you not read what was said to you by God: I am the God of Abraham, and the God of Isaac, and the God of Jacob'? He is not God of the dead, but of the living." And when the crowd heard it, they were astonished at his teaching.

(Matthew 22:30-33)

And Jesus said to them, "The sons of this age marry and are given in marriage, but those who are considered worthy to attain to that age and to the resurrection from the dead neither marry nor are given in marriage, for they cannot die anymore, because they are equal to angels and are sons of God, being sons of the resurrection. But that the dead are raised, even Moses showed, in the passage about the bush, where he calls the Lord the God of Abraham and the God of Isaac and the God of Jacob. Now he is not God of the dead, but of the living, for all live to him."

(Luke 20:34-38)

For none of us lives to himself, and none of us dies to himself. For if we live, we live to the Lord, and if we die, we die to the Lord. So then, whether we live or whether we die, we are the Lord's. For to this end Christ died and lived again, that he might be Lord both of the dead and of the living.

(Romans 14:7-9)

As I study this, I see the word resurrection used in a few ways. One way is when we physically die, our spirit rises into a new spiritual body, and we are with Jesus in heaven. So Jesus told the thief on the cross before they both died, 'today you will be with me in paradise.'

But the primary use is towards our new physical body, as what Jesus had when He appeared to the disciples:

As they were talking about these things, Jesus himself stood among them, and said to them, "Peace to you!" But they were startled and frightened and thought they saw a spirit. And he said to them, "Why are you troubled, and why do doubts arise in your hearts? See my hands and my feet, that it is I myself. Touch me, and see. For a spirit does not have flesh and bones as you see that I have." And when he had said this, he showed them his hands and his feet. And while they still disbelieved for joy and were marveling, he said to them, "Have you anything here to eat?" They gave him a piece of broiled fish, and he took it and ate before them.

(Luke 24:36-43)

SIDEBAR Five - Flesh and Bones.

God blessed me with a 30+ year career in sales. God provided success, and my wife and I were so blessed to have walked in what He has given us in this life. And one of the outcomes I received within my sales career was asking questions. So in reading the account above, I have questions.

Jesus appeared to His disciples. The disciples recognized Jesus. But they didn't see Him open the door; He just appeared! The first impulse was to say they all saw a 'spirit.' But Jesus knowing their hearts, still answered their thoughts.

He tells them to look at Him. Then, he shows them his scars. THEN he tells them to 'touch me.'

Then Jesus says: "For a spirit does not have flesh and bones, as you see that I have."

Whoa!?! Not flesh and blood, but flesh and bones. Reading this got me thinking.

Has the crimson redemption thread given throughout the bible - from God killing an animal for a covering of Adam and Eve as clothes [a sin covering metaphor]! From the animal sacrifices God required under the law. "To Jesus, the mediator of a new covenant, and to the sprinkled blood that speaks a better word than the blood of Abel." [Hebrews 12:24]. To Jesus' death on the cross, when the soldier pierced Jesus' side, and blood and water spilled to the ground – end with Jesus' resurrection? For "It is finished !" [John 19:30.] Does this mean that our resurrected bodies do not need blood to live - as Jesus appeared to His disciples. He declared to them that He is of 'flesh and bone?' Could the Holy Spirit now be our 'lifeblood' we need to live forever in our resurrected bodies? I am now intrigued to know if Jesus is offering us insights. I don't have a definitive answer for you or myself, but I currently am leaning toward – very possible!

I'm not smart enough to understand the question I ask, let alone find a definitive biblical answer.

However, I am compelled to take a theological risk in saying Jesus paid for everything. His blood finished the work of redemption for sin, and our resurrected bodies will be just like Jesus,' except with no scars or imperfections. Therefore, I lean heavily on what I know today to say that the Holy Spirit within us will sustain us in our resurrected bodies – FOREVER!

Spiritual bodies don't need blood, for we are alive by and through the Holy Spirit! So when Jesus returns to earth, He is in His resurrected body – for He has flesh and bone, as He tells His disciples. And in the twinkling of an eye, we will be just like Jesus.

Jesus also ate. So there is another question I can't answer. On the new earth, the tree of life will be there. And we know Jesus ate fish in His resurrected body. Will eating be for sustaining life or for the pleasure of taste? Will we who are in our resurrected bodies need food, or will we, the body of Christ, be sustained by the Holy Spirit? And – will eating food be for future Israel to partake?

> They shall build houses and inhabit them; they shall plant vineyards and eat their fruit.

> (Isaiah 65:21)

Our revisiting the verses to the tree of life declares that it will bear 12 different fruits per month [Revelation 22:2]. Is that tree for those of us in our resurrected bodies, or is this tree there for future Israel - born within the new Earth and Jerusalem? Another Hmmm.

But, when God calls me home one day, He will give me perfect wisdom - so it won't even matter, because I'll be with Him and find out as He has planned.

Connecting thoughts.

I see the Rapture and Resurrection having the same outcome, new immortal bodies coming out of our old mortal bodies.

I see the first fruits beginning with Jesus and flowing into the time of the Rapture as having a resurrected body.

In the resurrection of the dead, Jesus ties the Rapture to the end of the age. And He corrected the Sadducees – who did not believe in the resurrection, about their errors in understanding the OT scriptures.

There is the first resurrection, the resurrection of the saints. And then, later on, there is the second resurrection, for those without Christ who will enter judgment for their sins into eternal damnation.

So how does this all fit into Heaven today and my wife now living there?

Good question, thanks for asking.

She is living, yes, living with Jesus today, with all the other saints. And now, based on scripture, she is in her spiritual body, waiting for the will of God to reunite her with her new immortal body on the new Earth when Jesus returns.

CHAPTER 9

The Body of Christ – First Fruits of the Resurrection

Jesus.

But in fact Christ has been raised from the dead, the firstfruits of those who have fallen asleep.

(1 Corinthians 15:20)

But each in his own order: Christ the firstfruits, then at his coming those who belong to Christ.

(1 Corinthians 15:23)

As previously presented, Jesus has defeated sin and death, died for our sins, and risen again to life. Jesus is eternal, yet He died and rose in life for us!

I am the good shepherd. I know my own and my own know me, just as the Father knows me and I know the Father; and I lay down my life for the sheep. And I have other sheep that are not of this fold. I must bring them also, and they will listen to my voice. So there will be one flock, one shepherd. For this reason the Father loves me, because I lay down my life that I may take it up again. No one takes it from me, but I lay it down of my own accord. I have authority to lay it down, and I have authority to take it up again. This charge I have received from my Father."

(John 10:14-18)

We who believe. And who belong to Christ!

We who believe in Jesus as the Christ, the Son of the living God, have as evidence to our faith the Holy Spirit who lives within us - testifying with our spirit that we are His! Because of Jesus' finished work on the cross and His resurrection from the dead, we also live.

Christ, having been raised from the dead, IS the first fruit of the resurrection; for Jesus gives life. All who are in Christ. – those who belong to Him - are not of mortal flesh, but of His Spirit—pausing for a moment for prayer to ask for understanding.

> You, however, are not in the flesh but in the Spirit, if in fact the Spirit of God dwells in you. Anyone who does not have the Spirit of Christ does not belong to him. But if Christ is in you, although the body is dead because of sin, the Spirit is life because of righteousness. If the Spirit of him who raised Jesus from the dead dwells in you, he who raised Christ Jesus from the dead will also give life to your mortal bodies through his Spirit who dwells in you.

(Romans 8:9-11)

> But we ought always to give thanks to God for you, brothers beloved by the Lord, because God chose you as the firstfruits to be saved, through sanctification by the Spirit and belief in the truth.

(2 Thessalonians 2:13)

For we know that flesh and blood cannot inherit the Kingdom of God [1 Corinthians 15:50], but of and by the Holy Spirit, God changes us at the instant we die.

So now my wife Sandy, who lives with Jesus in Heaven, is a member of the first fruits of Christ. And all those of faith who come after her when they die will also be first fruits until Jesus returns for the Rapture of the saints, with our spirit bodies conjoining to a new immortal body.

If you have also read my first two books, you may see a pattern. I like to take scripture verses and write them out in an outline format. For it helps me better see the connections to the scriptures.

So let us look deeper at 1 Corinthians 15 and supportive verses to help further parse out the meaning.

I.   But in fact Christ has been raised from the dead,
    a.   The first fruits of those who have fallen asleep [died].
II. For as by a man came death [Adam],
    a.   By a man [Jesus] has come also the resurrection of the dead.
III. For as in Adam all die,
    a.   So also in Christ shall all be made alive.
        A.   Thus it is written, "The first man Adam became a living being;" the last Adam became a life-giving spirit. 1 Corinthians 15:45; For the bread of God is he who comes down from heaven and gives life to the world." John 6:33; And this is the will of him who sent me, that I should lose nothing of all that he has given me, but raise it up on the last day. John 6:39; Whoever feeds on my flesh and drinks my blood has eternal life, and I will raise him up on the last day. John 6:54; You, however, are not in the flesh but in the Spirit, if in fact the Spirit of God dwells in you. Anyone who does not have the Spirit of Christ does not belong to him. [10] But if Christ is in you, although the body is dead because of sin, the Spirit is life because of righteousness. [11] If the Spirit of him who raised Jesus from the dead dwells in

you, he who raised Christ Jesus from the dead will also give life to your mortal bodies through his Spirit who dwells in you. Romans 8:9-11

IV. But each in his own order: [Speaking to the Resurrection of the body]

   a. Christ the first fruits,

      A. then at his coming those who belong to Christ.

      B. Then comes the end, when he delivers the kingdom to God the Father

         1. after destroying every rule and every authority and power.

      C. For he must reign until he has put all his enemies under his feet.

      D. The last enemy to be destroyed is death.

      E. For "God has put all things in subjection under his feet."

         1. But when it says, "all things are put in subjection," it is plain that he is excepted who put all things in subjection under him.

      F. When all things are subjected to him,

         1. then the Son himself will also be subjected to him who put all things in subjection under him,

         2. that God may be all in all.   1 Corinthians 15:20-28

   b. We who believe are also first fruits:

But we ought always to give thanks to God for you, brothers beloved by the Lord, because God chose you as the first fruits to be saved, through sanctification by the Spirit and belief in the truth.   2 Thessalonians 2:13

So then the order is

      A. Christ is our [the] first fruit,

      B. Then we who believe in His coming, are also first fruits, [next in line].

      C. Then comes the end.

      D. In which Jesus must reign until

         1. All His enemies are under His feet,

         2. Then that includes the last enemy of death being destroyed.

3. Then when all things are under Christs subjection,
   a. Christ then will also be under God the Father's subjection
   b. And [He will] return the kingdom back to the Father.

Now, Paul continues about what type of body the resurrection will bring. Notice Paul starts with being of body and flesh as in being mortal; and body as in Heavenly. But for animals and birds and fish, he uses only flesh.

I. But someone will ask, "How are the dead raised?
II. With what kind of body do they come?"
   a. You foolish person!
      i. What you sow does not come to life unless it dies.
         1. And what you sow is not the body that is to be, but a bare kernel,
            a. Perhaps wheat or some other grain.
         2. But God gives it a body as he has chosen,
         3. And to each kind of seed its own body.
         4. For not all flesh is the same,
            a. But there is one kind for humans,
            b. another for animals,
            c. another for birds,
            d. and another for fish.
            e. There are Heavenly bodies
            f. and earthly bodies,
               i. but the glory of the Heavenly is of one kind,
               ii. and the glory of the Earthly is of another.
            g. There is one glory of the sun,
            h. and another glory of the moon,
            i. and another glory of the stars;
               i. for star differs from star in glory.

So remember the table in Chapter Eight?

   b. So is it with the resurrection of the dead.

   i. What is sown is perishable;

     1. Is raised is imperishable.

  ii. It is sown in dishonor;

     1. it is raised in glory.

 iii. It is sown in weakness;

     1. it is raised in power.

 iv. It is sown a natural body;

     1. it is raised a spiritual body.

  v. If there is a natural body,

     1. there is also a spiritual body.

 vi. Thus it is written, "The first man Adam became a living being;"

     1. the last Adam became a life-giving spirit.

 vii. But it is not the spiritual that is first but the natural,

     1. and then the spiritual.

viii. The first man was from the earth,

     1. a man of dust;

 ix. the second man is from Heaven.

  x. As was the man of dust,

     1. so also are those who are of the dust,

 xi. and as is the man of Heaven,

     1. so also are those who are of Heaven.

 xii. Just as we have borne the image of the man of dust,

     1. we shall also bear the image of the man of Heaven.

1 Corinthians 15:35-49

So let's continue.

I. I tell you this, brothers: flesh and blood cannot inherit the kingdom of God,

  a. nor does the perishable inherit the imperishable.

    i. Flesh and Blood is very significant. The mortal body {perishable} HAS to cease, so that the spiritual body {imperishable} emerges.

    ii. Jesus tells Nicodemus:

        1. Jesus answered, "Truly, truly, I say to you, unless one is born of water and the Spirit, he cannot enter the kingdom of God. John 3:5

    iii. Again where is the blood? Not flesh and blood but water and the Spirit!

II. Behold! I tell you a mystery. We shall not all sleep,

  a. but we shall all be changed,

  b. in a moment, in the twinkling of an eye,

  c. at the last trumpet. For the trumpet will sound,

    i. and the dead will be raised imperishable,

        1. {Dead, mortal bodies WILL BE raised imperishable} See iii.

    ii. and we shall be changed.

    iii. For this perishable body must put on the imperishable,

    iv. and this mortal body must put on immortality.

    v. When the perishable puts on the imperishable,

    vi. and the mortal puts on immortality,

        1. {This is a bit confusing to me, in that it seems it is stated backwards. Mortal body is replaced by Spiritual Body which later is conjoined with an immortal body at the rapture. Paul 'skips' the spiritual body with the intent to declare that having a physical body is our beginning and ultimately our ending point. This does not negate nor dimmish the 'absent from the body and present with the Lord of Heaven upon our last breath, but goes back to Paul's original statement that flesh and blood cannot inherit the kingdom of God.

        2. Jesus, after His resurrection, appeared to the disciples in the upper room. And the disciples thought Jesus was a spirit. HOWEVER, Jesus showed them His scares in His hands, and in His side, and he said, that He was Flesh and Bones. Not flesh and blood.

           a. As they were talking about these things, Jesus himself stood among them, and said to them, "Peace to you!"

But they were startled and frightened and thought they saw a spirit. And he said to them, "Why are you troubled, and why do doubts arise in your hearts? See my hands and my feet, that it is I myself. Touch me, and see. **For a spirit does not have flesh and bones as you see that I have**." And when he said this, he showed them his hands and his feet. And while they still disbelieved for joy and were marveling, he said to them, "Have you anything here to eat?" They gave him a piece of broiled fish, and he took it and ate before them. Luke 24:36-43

 b. I tell you this, brothers: flesh and blood cannot inherit the kingdom of God, nor does the perishable inherit the imperishable. 1 Corinthians 15:50

3. Question then is this. When Jesus shed His blood on the cross of pain and suffering, and in His resurrection - this satisfied the wrath of God for all who believe in Him. Being that Jesus' blood was poured out of him when the Roman Centurion pierced him, and the blood and water poured out from His body. And then when He arose, life to His body is through the Holy Spirit and not through blood, for the blood paid the price for our sins and is no longer life-giving in the resurrection. Jesus is.

 a. Thus it is written, "The first man Adam became a living being;" the last Adam became **a life-giving spirit**. 1 Corinthians 15:45

 b. Romans 8:9-11 You, however, are not in the flesh but in the Spirit, if in fact the Spirit of God dwells in you. Anyone who does not have the Spirit of Christ does not belong to him. But if Christ is in you, although the body is dead because of sin, the Spirit is life because of righteousness. If the Spirit of him who raised Jesus from the dead dwells in you, he who raised Christ Jesus from the dead will also give life to your mortal bodies through his Spirit who dwells in you.

vii. then shall come to pass the saying that is written:
    1. "Death is swallowed up in victory."
    2. "O death, where is your victory?
    3. O death, where is your sting?"
viii. The sting of death is sin,
    1. and the power of sin is the law.
ix. But thanks be to God, who gives us the victory
    1. through our Lord Jesus Christ.

1 Corinthians 15:50-57

CHAPTER 10

What Happens Next - After the Rapture?

Life keeps moving forward.

As we began our study, we looked at what happens at death for a Christian, using my wife, Sandy, as our guide through the verses of the Bible.

In review, God created us through the union of dad and mom; we are all conceived in sin, for this is our first birth - for we are born into a sinful, mortal, physical life first. And then, in this life, we who believe - are born-again by the Spirit of God through the grace and faith in Jesus given to us by God. Thus, begins our realized, eternal life in Christ; for we now have His Spirit living in us as we are part of the body of Christ.

So this is our second stage of life experience.

When this tent fails, Jesus receives us at our last breath, and we now live with Him, face-to-face, in our spiritual bodies, for which God declares that our spiritual body is our building, for spiritual, then overtakes mortal. 'That which is flesh is flesh. That which is spirit is spirit.' 'This Earth is not our home, for our citizenship is in Heaven.'

Our spiritual body becomes our third phase of life.

Then, to the time when God the Father says, 'it is time,' a war breaks out in Heaven between Michael and his angels with Satan and his angels. And Michael wins the battle, and Satan is 'kicked out of Heaven.' Naturally, this infuriates Satan, and he responds with wrath upon the Earth for a short season, as God allows. And as Satan is allowed to express his hate and anger on the world, God will cut this short by sending Jesus back to the world to give the saints their resurrected bodies, and to judge the world then.

Our newly resurrected, immortal, physical body completes the believers' stages of life eternal. Our resurrected bodies will be our fourth phase of life. God brings us into eternity, always with Him, from the day we first believed! As God has planned from the beginning. [Ephesians 1:3-10]

1. Mortal physical body,
2. To the indwelling of the Holy Spirit - being born-again. Our Spiritual Birth.
3. To realize life eternal in our spiritual body at our last breath – now in the presence of Jesus – with the surety of the Holy Spirit
4. To come in the clouds with Jesus, to receive our new resurrected immortal, eternal bodies – with our Spiritual bodies – still with the Holy Spirit living in us. – Note that the Holy Spirit never leaves us once we are born again. Not on this Earth, not when we are in Heaven, and not when we are in our resurrected bodies on the new Earth.

So the next question moves from living with Jesus in heaven to living with Jesus when He returns to Earth in Judgement.

So what happens next after the Rapture?

I could end and say all the saints live happily ever after. And we do, and it is proper. However, the Bible tells us more. Therefore, it is appropriate for me to present, for understanding, a few more events that God has declared within His word that affect those in Christ.

And to stay within the context of my wife and the saints' perspective of seeing eternal life through their experiences now, but bringing to light what the Bible says happens next after we receive our resurrected bodies.

Understanding a few critical eschatological points that many scholars have asked and even debated is prudent. The last chapters will present my understanding of our life in Jesus to the time of new Heaven, Earth, and New Jerusalem.

Within my second book, 'En Route to the Mount of Olives – Matthew 24,' I presented Jesus' answering the Disciples' two questions, 'what is the sign of your return, and what is the sign to the end of the age?' And to that, I declared what Jesus shared in His teachings. My heart was for the reader to know the times and signs, as Jesus warned in Matthew 24.

And now, within this study, my heart is to shine the light on God's word sitting over our life experiences, for we are His and not our own.

So starting from this point forward, my purpose and intent are to show two points God presents for a believer to understand what happens after our Rapture.

The first point is that the church is not the Bride of Jesus. Saved Israel is. And my second point is that Sandy, including all the saints - makes up the Body of Christ. Up and through the time of the Rapture.

In the first nine chapters, I presented what God has declared in life-to-life by seeing my wife go home and ask questions, exploring what God has revealed to life with Him in Heaven through the scriptures from the Bible.

Now, it's time to tie our experiences to the end of the age, to the New Heavens, New Earth, and New Jerusalem. Let us continue.

After Jesus returns to Earth, and when all the saints have received their new immortal resurrected bodies. What happens next?

A lot! And what I mean is a lot will happen on Earth next.

"Immediately after the tribulation of those days the sun will be darkened, and the moon will not give its light, and the stars will fall from heaven, and the powers of the heavens will be shaken. Then will appear in heaven the sign of the Son of Man, and then all the tribes of the earth will mourn, and they will see the Son of Man coming on the clouds of heaven with power and great glory. And he will send out his angels with a loud trumpet call, and they will gather his elect from the four winds, from one end of heaven to the other.

(Matthew 24:29-31)

When he opened the sixth seal, I looked, and behold, there was a great earthquake, and the sun became black as sackcloth, the full moon became like blood, and the stars of the sky fell to the earth as the fig tree sheds its winter fruit when shaken by a gale. The sky vanished like a scroll that is being rolled up, and every mountain and island was removed from its place. Then the kings of the earth and the great ones and the generals and the rich and the powerful, and everyone, slave and free, hid themselves in the caves and among the rocks of the mountains, calling to the mountains and rocks, "Fall on us and hide us from the face of him who is seated on the throne, and from the wrath of the Lamb, for the great day of their wrath has come, and who can stand?"

(Revelation 6:12-17)

The time is now for the wrath of God to begin. And for the Trumpet and Bowl Judgments - through to Jesus defeating the last enemy, death. But I am skipping over this period to speak next to the wedding of Jesus and the Bride.

So, Who is the Bride of Christ?

As I started my studies on what happens at death for a Christian, some of the verses I have known to support the understanding that the church is the Bride of Christ began to bother me. In my first book, 'The Sovereignty of God in Our Daily Lives,' I went back to see what I wrote, and sure enough - I declared that the bride of Jesus is the church [Pg 39].

And within my second book, En Route to the Mount of Olives, I carried that theme as a given, that Jesus is the husband to the bride as the church.

But as I started to dig deeper into the Word for this study, and through prayer and research, and as I read and reread the various traditional texts that many use in support, I am no longer quick to say so. I felt bothered. Maybe the wisdom of God by the Holy Spirit was tugging on me, showing the verses that didn't fit my current understanding.

For example, all the churches I have attended position the Bride of Christ as the church. Yet, as I now read and quote all these verses, I'm having difficulty 'owning' this as my doctrine.

Here is a brief synopsis of that teaching from gotquestions.org, summarizing what I first accepted.

> The imagery and symbolism of marriage is applied to Christ and the body of believers known as the church. The church is comprised of those who have trusted in Jesus Christ as their personal Savior and have received eternal life. Christ, the Bridegroom, has sacrificially and lovingly chosen the church to be His bride (Ephesians 5:25–27). Just as there was a betrothal period in biblical times during which the bride and groom were separated until the wedding, so is the bride of Christ separate from her Bridegroom during the church age. Her responsibility during the betrothal period is to be faithful to Him (2

Corinthians 11:2; Ephesians 5:24). At the rapture, the church will be united with the Bridegroom and the official "wedding ceremony" will take place and, with it, the eternal union of Christ and His bride will be actualized (Revelation 19:7–9; 21:1-2).

Gotquestions.org https://www.gotquestions.org/ bride-of-Christ.html Pulled 4/13/2022

For many years, I admittedly did not think much about the standard teaching of today - that the Church is the Bride of Christ. But through this study, I assumed incorrectly. Therefore, I should have taken the time to revisit this and to know what I believe, why I believe it, and that it aligns with the truth of the word, and then I can explain why I believe what I believe.

As I have come to study and learn, I now understand within Paul's writings that we are Jesus' Body, not His Bride. Therefore, I praise God for answering my prayer as I began drafting this book – that He would be our teacher and reveal my errors of assumption and grow me in Spirit and truth, which is my prayer for you as well.

Therefore, when we die in this life, we are absent from the body and instant with Jesus in our new spiritual bodies. And when Jesus returns to Earth, we will gather together with Jesus in the air as He returns and will be given our new resurrected immortal bodies, just like Jesus. And we are now always with Him as when we first became saved, for He did not leave us as orphans:

He indwells in us when we are born again.

We will see Him face-to-face in our spiritual bodies that emerges after our last breath. And we will always be with Him! First, in the Spirit at our second birth and then face-to-face at our last breath!

We are always with Him. Forever!

Now, suppose we are to be the Bride of Christ. And if we are the Bride, thus being the betrothed, are we to be separated from the Groom - as is the Jewish custom before the wedding? Does not the Spirit of Jesus live within us as we do in Him? Is Jesus not always with us? 2 Corinthians 5 says, 'absent from the body and now present with the Lord.' So I ask again, is the Church the Bride of Jesus?

As I started to dig deeper into the Bible, I could not locate any scriptures that declare that the Church is the Bride of Jesus. I feel somewhat humbled that I can't find the verses that say this if so, for I always assumed this was the case and took it for granted. The best I can find is stated in Revelation 19.

> Then I heard what seemed to be the voice of a great multitude, like the roar of many waters and like the sound of mighty peals of thunder, crying out,
>
> "Hallelujah! For the Lord our God the Almighty reigns. Let us rejoice and exult and give him the glory, for the marriage of the Lamb has come, **and his Bride has made herself ready; it was granted her to clothe herself with fine linen, bright and pure"**—for the fine linen is the **righteous deeds of the saints.**
>
> And the angel said to me, "Write this: Blessed are those who are invited to the marriage supper of the Lamb." And he said to me, "These are the true words of God." Then I fell down at his feet to worship him, but he said to me, "You must not do that! I am a fellow servant with you and your brothers who hold to the testimony of Jesus. Worship God." For the testimony of Jesus is the spirit of prophecy.
>
> (Revelation 19:6-10; emphasis added)

For the LORD has chosen Zion; he has desired it for his dwelling place: "This is my resting place forever; here I will dwell, for I have desired it. I will abundantly bless her provisions; I will satisfy her poor with bread. **Her priests I will <u>clothe with salvation</u>, and <u>her saints</u> will shout for joy.**

(Psalms 132:13-16; emphasis added)

[See Parking Lot 02 – The Bride of Christ, in the appendix for additional support.]

So then, who's the Bride?

CHAPTER 11

Is Saved Israel the Bride?

Then came one of the seven angels who had the seven bowls full of the seven last plagues and spoke to me, saying, "**Come, I will show you the Bride, the wife of the Lamb.**" And he carried me away in the Spirit to a great, high mountain, and showed me the holy city Jerusalem coming down out of heaven from God, having the glory of God, its radiance like a most rare jewel, like a jasper, clear as crystal. It had a great, high wall, with twelve gates, and at the gates twelve angels, and on the gates the names of the twelve tribes of the sons of Israel were inscribed— on the east three gates, on the north three gates, on the south three gates, and on the west three gates. And the wall of the city had twelve foundations, and on them were the twelve names of the twelve apostles of the Lamb.

(Revelation 21:9-14; emphasis added)

Is this the New Jerusalem? A city as the Bride?

Then I saw a new heaven and a new earth, for the first heaven and the first earth had passed away, and the sea was no more. And I saw the holy city, new Jerusalem, coming down out of heaven from God, **prepared as a bride adorned for her husband**. And I heard a loud voice from the throne saying, "Behold, the dwelling place of

God is with man. He will dwell with them, and they will be his people, and God himself will be with them as their God. He will wipe away every tear from their eyes, and death shall be no more, neither shall there be mourning, nor crying, nor pain anymore, for the former things have passed away."

And he who was seated on the throne said, "Behold, I am making all things new." Also he said, "Write this down, for these words are trustworthy and true." And he said to me, "It is done! I am the Alpha and the Omega, the beginning and the end.

(Revelation 21:1-6; emphasis added)

Could this be saved Israel when the new Jerusalem comes down from above?

I will greatly rejoice in the LORD; my soul shall exult in my God, for he has clothed me with the garments of salvation; he has covered me with the robe of righteousness, as a bridegroom decks himself like a priest with a beautiful headdress, and as a bride adorns herself with her jewels. For as the earth brings forth its sprouts, and as a garden causes what is sown in it to sprout up, so the Lord GOD will cause righteousness and praise to sprout up before all the nations.

(Isaiah 61:10-11; emphasis added)

Then I looked, and behold, on Mount Zion stood the Lamb, and with him 144,000 who had his name and his Father's name written on their foreheads. And I heard a voice from heaven like the roar of many waters and like the sound of loud thunder. The voice I heard was like the sound of harpists playing on their harps, and they were singing a new song before the throne and before the four living creatures and before the elders. **No one could learn that song except the 144,000 who had been redeemed from the earth**. It is these who have not defiled themselves with women, for they are virgins. **It is these who follow the Lamb wherever he goes. These have been redeemed from mankind as firstfruits for God and the Lamb**, and in their mouth no lie was found, for they are blameless.

(Revelation 14:1-5; emphasis added)

For who is the greater, one who reclines at table or one who serves? Is it not the one who reclines at table? But I am among you as the one who serves.

"You are those who have stayed with me in my trials, and I assign to you, as my Father assigned to me, a kingdom, that you may eat and drink at my table in my kingdom and sit on thrones judging the twelve tribes of Israel.

(Luke 22:27-30)

I need to pause and reread the above, starting with - "Come, I show you the Bride, the wife of the Lamb."

What I do not see is any reference to the church. Nor do I see a direct statement toward Jewish Israel. But of the coming down of the new Jerusalem. And to the respects to the twelve gates, twelve tribes of Israel, and the twelve Apostles.

But adding further, we now see 'the 144,000' people. NOW is the time for Israel's salvation. Notice that Jesus is here and now on Earth, and the 144,000 have become saved! So the Court of Heaven, sans Jesus – who is on earth, rejoice! John declares: "The voice I heard was like the sound of harpists playing on their harps, and they were singing a new song before the throne and before the four living creatures and before the elders."

So let us go back to confirm that the church is not the Bride of Christ; that the angel is telling John.

Ephesians 5:31-32 Revisited.

"Therefore a man shall leave his father and mother and hold fast to his wife, and the two shall become one flesh." This mystery is profound, and I am saying that it refers to Christ and the church.

Once again, Ephesians 5:31-32 presents the mystery of marriage as a model of Christ and the Church. When we understand the Gospel, God brings us from spiritual death to spiritual life. So we are in Christ, and He is in us! Therefore, we are born-again! Not betrothed for marriage, but born-again by the Holy Spirit the day we first believed.

For the husband is the head of the wife even as Christ is the head of the church, his body, and is himself its Savior.

(Ephesians 5:23)

Paul says the mystery is not that the church will be Jesus' bride, but that it is Jesus' body, and that Jesus is its Savior! Jesus is the head of the body [of Christ!]

And when the Rapture happens, all the saints who died before the church age are also given new resurrected bodies. Therefore, the saints in heaven and the saints who remain here on this Earth are the body of Jesus. Those Old Testament saints predated their time on Earth before Jesus established the church, but are in Christ nonetheless, for they looked forward to the promise. So if only the church were the bride of Christ, then the Old Testament saints would be left out.

> These all died in faith, not having received the things promised, but having seen them and greeted them from afar, and having acknowledged that they were strangers and exiles on the earth.

> (Hebrews 11:13)

I now submit for your continued consideration that the church cannot be the Bride of Jesus, for God places us in the body of Christ, with Jesus as the head as a husband is the head of his wife. Positionally and literally. Jesus is our Savior to the Old and New Testament saints alike. We all are alive in Christ! For He lives in us as we live in Him!

There is no segregation in Heaven between Old and New Testament saints. They [We] are one in Christ and counted as one when the Rapture happens.

And most importantly, all are in Heaven - within their spiritual bodies. At the Rapture, all will be given their resurrected bodies and will always be physically and spiritually with Christ.

> For the Lord himself will descend from heaven with a cry of command, with the voice of an archangel, and with the sound of the trumpet of God. **And the dead in Christ will rise first.** Then we who are alive, who are left, will be caught up together with them in the clouds to meet the Lord in the air, **and so we will always be with the Lord.**

> (1 Thessalonians 4:16-17; emphasis added)

How then does Ephesians 5:31-32 fit or relate to Revelation 21:9-14?

So who is "the Bride, the Wife of the Lamb?" The Church? All the saints before the Rapture? Israel? The New Jerusalem? What do you think? Then what do you believe?

What I am saying and typing may be controversial - where there are centuries of steadfast understandings by the churches around me that declare that the Church is the Bride of Christ. But in studying the Word, I am convinced that the Church is the body of Christ, and that Saved Israel is His bride.

> "And in that day, declares the LORD, you will call me 'My Husband,' and no longer will you call me 'My Baal.' For I will remove the names of the Baals from her mouth, and they shall be remembered by name no more. And I will make for them a covenant on that day with the beasts of the field, the birds of the heavens, and the creeping things of the ground. And I will abolish the bow, the sword, and war from the land, and I will make you lie down in safety. And I will betroth you to me forever. I will betroth you to me in righteousness and in justice, in steadfast love and in mercy. I will betroth you to me in faithfulness. And you shall know the LORD.
>
> (Hosea 2:16-20)

I realize that this may go against the teaching of many Church denominations of today - as declared within their statements of faith. Many churches believe that the Church is the 'new' Israel.

But through the indwelling of the Holy Spirit, who is my ultimate teacher, and as I pray and study to own what I believe and search for that one meaning of the sum of thy word is truth, I'm standing on the word of God.

And it says that Christ is the head of the Church, as a husband is his wife's head. So my hesitancy is not to rush in to declare a new understanding but to present the scriptures for myself and the reader for your knowledge.

So in my heart, I see Paul declaring that Christ and the Church are as marriage is to a husband and wife. Jesus is the head, and we are His body, as he also writes in his letters to the Church at Corinth. And nothing more implied.

The Church is the place of the Christian congregation while on Earth – waiting and praying for Jesus' return. It is our place to worship corporately, witness, train, uphold, and support the body of Christ. For individuals born again in Christ, well, we are in Christ! He is our Lord and Savior, as His Spirit lives in us - forever!

The universal church breaks/transcends denominations and doctrinal misunderstandings. But God's grace through faith delivered by His Spirit in changing our hearts - brings us to understanding the Gospel. Again:

> For God, who said, "Let light shine out of darkness," has shone in our hearts to give the light of the knowledge of the glory of God in the face of Jesus Christ.
>
> (2 Corinthians 4:6)

The Church, the elect, the true believers in Christ, are His body, and He is in us, and we are in Him.

The nation of Israel, beginning from the time of Jesus' Second Coming - the 144,000 from the twelve tribes - is protected from the Great Tribulation. Those Jews who come through the Great Tribulation while guarded by God will then be with Jesus. Therefore, I lean to say that they are the first fruits of the salvation of the nation Israel. And to Israel of this day, she is the betrothed in view, as she will become the bride of Christ - if the bride is not the New Jerusalem.

"O Jerusalem, Jerusalem, the city that kills the prophets and stones those who are sent to it! How often would I have gathered your children together as a hen gathers her brood under her wings, and you were not willing! See, your house is left to you desolate. For I tell you, you will not see me again, until you say, Blessed is he who comes in the name of the Lord.'"

(Matthew 23:37-39)

Let us look again.

Then came one of the seven angels who had the seven bowls full of the seven last plagues and spoke to me, saying, "Come, I will show you the Bride, the wife of the Lamb." And he carried me away in the Spirit to a great, high mountain, and showed me the holy city Jerusalem coming down out of heaven from God,

(Revelation 21:9-10)

Whew! So is the Bride the city or the people within Jerusalem? Or do you still see the Bride as the Church? I will leave it there for you and the Spirit of God to understand.

Rabbit Trail Five: Ephesians 5 Deeper Dive.

I want to go back one more time to Ephesians 5, but this time with a different perspective.

Reviewing Genesis from chapters one and two, God created all things. Then He created Adam. And God did so from the dust of the ground.

Then the LORD God formed the man of dust from the ground and breathed into his nostrils the breath of life, and the man became a living creature. And the LORD God planted a garden in Eden, in the east, and there he put the man whom he had formed.

(Genesis 2:7-8)

Now, look at how God created Eve. From Adam's rib and not from the grounds dust.

The man gave names to all livestock and to the birds of the heavens and to every beast of the field. But for Adam there was not found a helper fit for him. So the LORD God caused a deep sleep to fall upon the man, and while he slept took one of his ribs and closed up its place with flesh. And the rib that the LORD God had taken from the man he made into a woman and brought her to the man. Then the man said,

"This at last is bone of my bones and flesh of my flesh; she shall be called Woman, because she was taken out of Man."

Therefore a man shall leave his father and his mother and hold fast to his wife, <u>and they shall become one flesh.</u>

(Genesis 2:20-24; emphasis added)

Please inspect this closely and note that God created Eve from man, Adam – 'bone of my bones and flesh of my flesh.' And the two are one. God made, or best word, created Eve, not from the dust, but out of Adam. All the other living creatures God made, He made males and females simultaneously. But for man, God formed man from the ground, breathed life into him, and later made a woman from man. And adding, for man. And to the church, those in Christ, for Christ.

Father, I desire that they also, whom you have given me, may be with me where I am, to see my glory that you have given me because you loved me before the foundation of the world.

(John 17:24)

So in correlation, the Church is the body of Christ. The Spirit of Christ saves those who believe, giving us eternal life, and we are His collective body as He is the head. The church functions here on this Earth in anticipation of Jesus' glorious return. And we are not orphans, for His Spirit lives within us. Those in Heaven and those on Earth in Christ will see Him face-to-face, either at the time of one's last breath or when He returns to Earth, giving us our resurrected, immortal bodies.

I hope that this helps fill in the gaps.

And remember, we who believe are joined to the Lord and become one spirit with Him.

Or do you not know that your body is a temple of the Holy Spirit within you, whom you have from God? You are not your own, for you were bought with a price. So glorify God in your body.

(1 Corinthians 6:17, 19-20)

CHAPTER 12

The Parable of the Wedding Feast.

I now present a rebuttal to the traditional arguments of Matthew 22, to the conventional, contemporary pretribulation understanding of today's church use of these verses in support of the Bride as the subject, and the object is the Church.

I don't see this as so. But I realize that many do. So in love for the Lord and people, and getting to that one meaning of scripture, I present the counterargument that Matthew 22 is not about the Bride of Jesus is the Church, but of Jesus' righteousness – in and through the wedding garment. And please make the distinction that it is not the wedding gown. This garment is akin to putting on the wedding attire the king offers each guest. [See Isaiah 61:10a quoted later below.]

> And again Jesus spoke to them in parables, saying, "The kingdom of heaven may be compared to a king who gave a wedding feast for his son, and sent his servants to call those who were invited to the wedding feast, but they would not come. Again he sent other servants, saying, 'Tell those who are invited, "See, I have prepared my dinner, my oxen and my fat calves have been slaughtered, and everything is ready. Come to the wedding feast."' But they paid no attention and went off, one to his farm, another to his business, while the rest seized his servants, treated them shamefully, and killed them. The king was angry, and he sent his troops and destroyed those murderers

and burned their city. Then he said to his servants, 'The wedding feast is ready, but those invited were not worthy. Go therefore to the main roads and invite to the wedding feast as many as you find.' And those servants went out into the roads and gathered all whom they found, both bad and good. So the wedding hall was filled with guests.

"But when the king came in to look at the guests, he saw there a man who had no wedding garment. And he said to him, Friend, how did you get in here without a wedding garment?' And he was speechless. Then the king said to the attendants, 'Bind him hand and foot and cast him into the outer darkness. In that place there will be weeping and gnashing of teeth.' For many are called, but few are chosen."

(Matthew 22:1-14)

Jesus tells us about the entry into The Kingdom at the end of Matthew 22 in verse 14. "For many are called, but few are chosen." And this is regarding the Kingdom of Heaven.

So is this parable about:

A. Who is the Bride?
B. The King's son getting married?
C. The guests snubbing the King's invitation to his son's wedding?
D. The King's anger against the guests who did not respond, then and then the killed his servants?
E. The other guests the King has invited?
F. The one guest without wearing a wedding garment?
G. A little bit of all the above?

I don't think it is option A, for the Bride is not stated within Jesus' story, or for who the Bride is, is not the subject or even the object of the story.

159

The King's son is - as is the wedding dinner leading to those invited. All are leading back to the kingdom of Heaven.

Outside of answer A, I see Jesus has a bit of B, C, D, E, and F in view. Let's examine it more closely.

- The King is planning a wedding feast for his son.
- The King has a guest list.
- The King sends his first servants to invite his 'people' directly, and those on the list give no attention and thus decline to come to the wedding.
- The King then sends another group of his servants to them, making his point well known. And instead of these guests RSVPing and attending, they again snubbed the King's invitation and went their ways - some even killed the King's servants.
- The King was furious when he found out, and He responded in wrath to those who murdered his servants, and the King's soldiers killed those invitees who killed his servants.
- Then the King sent the last group of his servants into the main streets – and he told his servant to bring anyone and everyone, for the invitation was no longer in the King's original guest list but to an open door.

Alas, the wedding hall is now filled with guests from the streets of the King's cities. Both the good and the bad.

- The King enters the room to check out his invitees and sees that the room is full of guests.
- Now, he notices the attire of one particular guest. This man was so out of place because of his clothes – for he lacked a wedding garment. The implication is that everyone else was attired correctly, putting on their wedding garments that the King supplied.
- Notice that it doesn't say this one man was good or bad but lacked wearing a wedding garment.

y4

- Remember - the hall now is filled with people. Nowhere does Jesus say that these people are the Bride. They were guests of the King at his son's wedding.
- And one guest was not properly attired.
- Now the King goes to this man directly and asks him, "Friend, how did you get in here without a wedding garment?'
- Friend? The King warmly calls this man a friend. A term of endearment, of relationship, of familiarity.
- Ah ha. Getting into the wedding hall as a king's guest required having the proper attire to enter.
- "And this man was speechless when asked. Then the King said to the attendants, 'Bind him hand and foot, and cast him into the outer darkness. In that place, there will be weeping and gnashing of teeth.' For many are called, but few are chosen."
- Why was he speechless?
- Here are the key points I see. The King has a son who is getting married. The King invites his friends from his guest list. Those named on the King's list snub the wedding/snubs the King – and they do this twice. And some on the list even killed the King's servants. The King is furious with those he has invited. And the soldiers of the King kill those who killed his servants. The wedding will still happen, so the King invites anyone and everyone. The banquet hall is complete, the marriage is about to happen, and one guest has not dressed appropriately. The entrance requirement of the attendees required proper attire. And when the King asked how this man came to be in the room without a wedding garment, the man was speechless! Thus, the King judged him unfit to be there.
- The question was not how he got into the King's banquet hall, but where was his wedding garment!
- What was the King's reply to the no-reply of the man without a wedding garment? The King had this man bound and banished from his banquet hall and his kingdom. And he was thrown into outer darkness.
- Wow!

Oh my, that had the Pharisees hopping mad.

> When the chief priests and the Pharisees heard his parables, they perceived that he was speaking about them. And although they were seeking to arrest him, they feared the crowds, because they held him to be a prophet.
>
> (Matthew 21:45-46)

So who is the bride? Jesus never states who is the bride; for this is not part of the parable. It is about righteousness—the righteous garment of the King. And the Pharisees knew it! But they didn't connect the dots. Because if they had, they would have acknowledged that this is about Jesus, His righteousness, and their unrighteousness.

For the meaning, had they known and understood the scriptures, they would have connected, that the guest was Israel (themselves), the servants were the Prophets, the invitation was to Israel, they rejected his invite, and is now open to anyone and everyone – with a catch. The wedding garment is the righteousness of Christ.

> I will greatly rejoice in the LORD; my soul shall exult in my God, for he has clothed me with the garments of salvation; he has covered me with the robe of righteousness,
>
> (Isaiah 61:10a)

> I put on righteousness, and it clothed me; my justice was like a robe and a turban.
>
> (Job 29:14)

Matthew writes to a highly Jewish audience. Jesus said that the kingdom of Heaven is through himself, that God invited you as God's [chosen] guests, and yet, you declined. And God's wrath came to the invitees, for they killed the King's servants.

And in their rejection, this opened the door to everyone and anyone. So all are now invited, the good and the bad. But there is only one stipulation-God's righteousness - you had to put on the wedding garment. So the King supplied everything the guests needed to participate in his son's wedding feast, even the wedding garment. But in the parable, this one man didn't put on his. And he was speechless when confronted as to why. Thus, the King's wrath and judgment fell upon him as well.

From The International Christian Embassy Jerusalem:

"This moment of inspection of the wedding garments is very instructive! The Fall festivals – Rosh Hashana, Yom Kippur and Feast of Tabernacles – are all tied together and all portend the Second Coming of Jesus! They speak prophetically of the Coronation of Jesus as King and the Wedding Feast of the Lamb.

The Parable of the Wedding Feast assumes the listener is familiar with the ancient Oriental custom of the host providing garments for the guests who were invited to a royal feast. In ancient times, kings and wealthy men had wardrobes filled with fancy garments (today called 'caftans') as a symbol of their wealth and glory. Examples can be found as follows:

Genesis 45:22 – Joseph gives all his brother garments, but three garments to Benjamin.

Judges 14:12 – Samson offers 30 linen garments and 30 changes of clothes to answer his riddle.

2 Kings 5:22 – Naaman promises 10 garments plus gold and silver to Elisha.

2 Kings 10:22 – King Jehu gives vestments from wardrobe in the temple of Baal.

Esther 6:8 and 8:15 – Haman says: "dress him in royal robes" / Mordechai is the one dressed in royal apparel.

Even today, at very posh country clubs and restaurants, there are similar strict dress codes, and small closets with appropriate dinner jackets and other attire if an improperly dressed guest warrants entry.

In the parable of Jesus, it would have been a great insult to the king to refuse to wear the garments freely offered to the guests. The man who was caught wearing his old clothing learned what an offense it was as he was forcefully removed from the celebration.

This was Jesus' way of teaching the inadequacy of self-righteousness. From the very beginning, God provided a "covering" for our sin. Adam and Eve tried to cover their nakedness and shame with fig leaves, but God replaced them with skins of animals, which meant a life had been sacrificed (Genesis 3:7, 21). To insist on covering our shame ourselves is to be clad in "filthy rags" (Isaiah 64:6). In the book of Revelation, we see those in heaven wearing "white robes" (Revelation 7:9), and we learn that the whiteness of the robes is due to their being washed in the blood of the Lamb (verse 14). We trust in God's righteousness, not our own (Philippians 3:9). Further, the true Church is described as "not having spot, or wrinkle" (Ephesians 5:27).

Finally, in Revelation 19:6-9, a great multitude has gathered for the "marriage of the Lamb ... and His wife has made herself ready. And to her it was granted to be arrayed in fine linen, clean and bright, for the fine linen is the righteous acts of the saints. Then he said to me, "Write: 'Blessed are those who are called to the marriage supper of the Lamb!"'" [*Yom Kippur: A Day to Prepare our Wedding Garments*, International Christian Embassy Jerusalem: Pulled 04-22-2022 https://int.icej.org/news/headlines/yo m-kippur-day-prepare-our-wedding-garments,]

'Blessed are those who are called to the marriage supper of the Lamb!'

Now, let's take a quick look at the faith of a Roman Soldier compared to the faith of Israel.

> When he had entered Capernaum, a centurion came forward to him, appealing to him, "Lord, my servant is lying paralyzed at home, suffering terribly." And he said to him, "I will come and heal him." But the centurion replied, "Lord, I am not worthy to have you come under my roof, but only say the word, and my servant will be healed. For I too am a man under authority, with soldiers under me. And I say to one, 'Go,' and he goes, and to another, 'Come,' and he comes, and to my servant, 'Do this,' and he does it." When Jesus heard this, he marveled and said to those who followed him, "Truly, I tell you, with no one in Israel have I found such faith. I tell you, many will come from east and west and recline at table with Abraham, Isaac, and Jacob in the kingdom of heaven, **while the sons of the kingdom will be thrown into the outer darkness. In that place there will be weeping and gnashing of teeth."**

> (Matthew 8:5-12; emphasis added)

So notice again that Jesus was hitting, and hitting hard on the religion of the Pharisees and of Israel. That faith in Jesus by a Roman Centurion overshadowed that of Israel.

So let us move to close the door, that the church is not the Bride.

CHAPTER 13

The Bride of Christ Summary

We, the born-again believers of Jesus, the ones clothed in Jesus' righteousness, and are the Body of Christ, have His Spirit living in us, as we also live in Him. Eve came from Adam. Therefore, Adam is the head of Eve. So a husband and wife represent Christ and the Church that Paul writes about; whereas from Adam comes Eve, as Adam is the head of Eve. And from Jesus comes the Body.

The Church, whereas Christ is the head of the Church - has a union with Jesus, as Eve has a union with Adam.

Stay with me, for this can get a bit complex. God created Eve from the rib of Adam. In the relationship of a man and a woman, Eve is [out] of Adam. And from Adam, she is part of him - but separated from him. Through marriage, that separation becomes a union or a reunion, for God made Eve from Adam, and they are known as one through marriage.

Still with me? So as with Jesus and the Holy Spirit. Christ is in us, as we are in Christ. Being born-again has the Spirit of God residing in us, as we are of Christ. Do not read that we are little christs, but that Jesus is in us. As Eve is a woman and not a man, God created her from one of Adam's ribs, and then, through marriage to Adam, they are identified in oneness. Therefore, in the same relationship, we who believe are of Jesus, and He is in us. Both Eve and the Body of Christ are in connection to the head, Adam to Eve, as Jesus is to the Body of believers. We are out of Jesus as the woman is out of the man. Separate yet connected. In marriage | in salvation.

Thus it is written, "The first man Adam became a living being;" the last Adam became a life-giving spirit. But it is not the spiritual that is first but the natural, and then the spiritual. The first man was from the earth, a man of dust; the second man is from heaven. As was the man of dust, so also are those who are of the dust, and as is the man of heaven, so also are those who are of heaven.

(1 Corinthians 15:45-48)

But God, being rich in mercy, because of the great love with which he loved us, even when we were dead in our trespasses, **made us alive together** *with Christ*—by grace you have been saved— and raised us up with him and seated us with him in the heavenly places in Christ Jesus, so that in the coming ages he might show the immeasurable riches of his grace in kindness toward us in Christ Jesus. For by grace you have been saved through faith. And this is not your own doing; it is the gift of God, not a result of works, so that no one may boast. For we are his workmanship, created in Christ Jesus for good works, which God prepared beforehand, that we should walk in them. (Ephesians 2:4-10; emphasis added)

But our citizenship is in heaven, and from it we await a Savior, the Lord Jesus Christ, who will transform our lowly body to be like his glorious body, by the power that enables him even to subject all things to himself.

(Philippians 3:20-21)

"Therefore a man shall leave his father and mother and hold fast to his wife, and the two shall become one flesh."

This mystery is profound, and I am saying that it refers to Christ and the church.

(Ephesians 5:31-32)

So why is this important? Because when we die, we will see Jesus face-to-face and be before Him forever. But Jesus has always been with us from the day of our salvation, for His Spirit lives within us, for as He stated, He didn't leave us as orphans.

In the previous life and place stages chapters, I have presented, by example, my wife Sandy and all the saints of Heaven, and the saints alive on the Earth at the Rapture will arrive next towards the New Earth when Christ returns – in our resurrected bodies.

We are not waiting to be married to Jesus, for we are already with and in Jesus as He is with and in us. At best, we would be the guests at the wedding of Jesus and Israel, who come to believe in Christ at the end of the age.

> "And in that day, declares the LORD, **you will call me 'My Husband,'** and no longer will you call me 'My Baal.' For I will remove the names of the Baals from her mouth, and they shall be remembered by name no more. And I will make for them a covenant on that day with the beasts of the field, the birds of the heavens, and the creeping things of the ground. And I will abolish the bow, the sword, and war from the land, and I will make you lie down in safety. **And I will betroth you to me forever. I will betroth you to me in righteousness and in justice, in steadfast love and in mercy. I will betroth you to me in faithfulness. And you shall know the LORD.**

(Hosea 2:16-20; emphasis added)

CHAPTER 14

So How do I Close?

A good salesperson would use his ABCs – Always Be Closing. Repetition helps convey and confirm - that the message sent is the message received—repetition brings understanding, leading to confirmation, then agreement.

So here goes my best attempt to cement that when we die, we are face-to-face with Jesus and are always with Jesus, and as such, He never leaves us.

From the vantage point of my wife, Sandy, with Scripture in support, she is now with Jesus. She can now be called one of the saints in Heaven. [You and I who believe we are also saints while living on Earth, too]. When her life was complete on this Earth, she passed from life to life—moving from a mortal, perishable body to a spiritual body pushing through at her last breath.

Sandy was born again to the work of the Holy Spirit's calling her to and through faith in 1972. And in life, God sanctified her to the faith He gave her as she walked in the good works; He had prepared for her to walk in - until her mission was complete, and God called her home. And with Jesus' Spirit living within her, she now lives with Jesus in Heaven today.

And in Heaven, she is in community, for we learned that God would give us perfect understanding in Heaven. Our heart's desire in Heaven is genuine love and adoration for the Glory of Jesus. And there will be things to do in Heaven, and may I add, unique to Heaven.

And she will remember her time of life on Earth. Sandy will know - and be known - for how she lived life on Earth and for the good works that God had her to walk in.

And to our family in heaven, she will see those family members who are also in Christ again. And I presented a high probability that there will be praises to Jesus in the reunion! During these times, the family celebrated in and through prayers while on Earth. Their praise and adoration continue toward Jesus for their salvation and those of family. And to thank and praise God for the times of His rescue, healing, and blessings. And for her prayers toward the needs of others. And just pure praises to be in the glory of Christ!

And as with Abraham and Lazarus - who saw and related with the rich man now in Hades, she should also have the same view. Whoa, to those who can only glimpse the paradise of Heaven, if Jesus' example within Abraham, Lazarus, and the rich man holds as an example. I continue to pray for the future generations of our family that God would save all generations from Sandy and me, for Jesus' name sake and glory, and for our eternal joy in living with Jesus in eternal worship.

As the author of Hebrews also writes, the 'great cloud of witnesses may very well be our loved ones in heaven, being able to watch in silent encouragement as we run our races to the finish line of faith, just like they did.

And she will be herself. And, as God created her as she appeared on Earth, she will still be known in the same appearance and personality in heaven. So, in her spiritual body, she still is as to what she 'looked' like on earth. But without imperfections. All ailments, scars, and deformities are gone! [No more stuck-together toes!] And in her spiritual body, she will wear clothes, clothed in white, as the robe of Christ's righteousness is upon her.

And in identity, Abraham, Lazarus, and the rich man knew each other. And to the rich man, his spiritual body felt pain, anguish, and thirst. The rich man's deeds, lack of compassion, and self-satisfying life cost him his eternal life - and he and Abraham and Lazarus remembered this.

And also, note that when Abraham stated why the rich man was not in heaven but tormented in Hades, the rich man did not repent. That when one dies, the time of repentance vanishes. Without faith in Christ before death is without Christ after ones death!

When Christ returns to Earth, so will those in Heaven.

When Jesus returns to Earth - both the saints in heaven and those alive on this Earth will physically meet Jesus in the clouds - now in our new, resurrected, immortal, eternal bodies. Bodies just like Jesus,' of flesh and bone. And praise God, we will be with Jesus in our resurrected bodies – forever! As with all saints, Sandy is now one of the first fruits of the resurrection. The Bride of Christ is yet to come; but we - those of us of the Rapture, are not the Bride. We are part of the body of Christ, now and forever!

And as we explored, I believe Jesus doesn't return twice; once to take the saints back to heaven in their resurrected bodies, and then return a second time in judgment. Instead, scripture states once, coming in the clouds. So the saints will always be with Jesus.

As to the wedding of Jesus, one of the critical markers, the Church is not the Bride of Christ, is our always being with Jesus!

The custom of a Jewish wedding is for the Groom to be away from his Bride before their wedding.

Many folks, and in my opinion, misinterpret John 14:3, when Jesus says: "And if I go and prepare a place for you, I will come again, and will take you to myself, that where I am you may be also."

Jesus is not speaking of the Wedding of the Church, but of the Cross of Pain and Suffering.

So, Jesus is saying that He must fulfill Scripture and that His death and resurrection must happen soon. Which Jesus is telling them is coming now. So, this is how He prepares a place for us. And actually, Jesus doesn't have the rooms of heaven in top-of-mind, but of Himself!

Because of the finished work of Christ, we now are received by HIMSELF when we breathe our last breath. All believers are the Body of Christ, not the future Bride of Christ! [Therefore, I again see Scripture pointing to the Bride as saved Jerusalem - Israel, not the Church! "And I will betroth you to me forever. I will betroth you to me in righteousness and injustice, in steadfast love and in mercy. I will betroth you to me in faithfulness. And you shall know the LORD." Hosea 2:19-20]

> So we, though many, are one body in Christ, and individually members one of another.
>
> (Romans 12:5)

> There is one body and one Spirit—just as you were called to the one hope that belongs to your call— one Lord, one faith, one baptism, one God and Father of all, who is over all and through all and in all.
>
> (Ephesians 4:4-6)

> Therefore do not be ashamed of the testimony about our Lord, nor of me his prisoner, but share in suffering for the gospel by the power of God, who saved us and called us to a holy calling, not because of our works but because of his own purpose and grace, which he gave us in Christ Jesus before the ages began, and which now has been manifested through the appearing of our Savior Christ Jesus, who abolished death and brought life and immortality to light through the gospel,
>
> (2 Timothy 1:8-10)

And we know that the Son of God has come and has given us understanding, so that we may know him who is true; and we are in him who is true, in his Son Jesus Christ. He is the true God and eternal life.

(1 John 5:20)

If you made it this far, congratulations are in order! I hope that through this study, God moved you as He moved me by the Holy Spirit as we studied His word together to learn more about eternity with Jesus than when we started.

What I didn't offer within this book was what happens to nonbelievers in Jesus when they also die, for my assumption was that this book will be read by those who have faith in Jesus Christ as your Lord and Savior.

It will be a bad thing—a horrible thing, an awful thing that is no longer irrevocable after your last breath if the Spirit of Jesus is not within you!

You, too, will continue to live in eternity if you are without Christ. And you will go through all the same stages of bodily life as a believer: that of mortal, spiritual, and immortal. But with one GIGANTIC exception - you will be in the wrath of God and judgment ... forever!

Hell and Hades will greet you in your spiritual body at your last breath, and the Lake of Fire and Sulfur will be your eternal destination at the end of the age when judgment happens at the second resurrection:

Then I saw a great white throne and him who was seated on it. From his presence earth and sky fled away, and no place was found for them. And I saw the dead, great and small, standing before the throne, and books were opened. Then another book was opened, which is the book of life. And the dead were judged by what was written in the books, according to what they had done. And the sea gave up the dead who were in it, Death and Hades gave up the

dead who were in them, and they were judged, each one
of them, according to what they had done. Then Death
and Hades were thrown into the lake of fire. This is the
second death, the lake of fire. And if anyone's name was
not found written in the book of life, he was thrown into
the lake of fire.

(Revelation 20:11-15)

Oh, I pray that this is not you. BUT, maybe as you were reading, God
opened your heart as you turned the pages, seeing the verses of the Gospel
before you 'pop' to you in wisdom and understanding of the Gospel of
Salvation. Is it too late to repent and believe? NO! Now is the day of
salvation. Now is the time!

Then he brought them out and said, "Sirs, what must I do
to be saved?" And they said, "Believe in the Lord Jesus,
and you will be saved, you and your household."

(Acts 16:30-31)

So in the grace of God giving you faith, if this makes sense to you - now
believe!

༄

"But the word of the Lord remains forever."
And this word is the good news that was preached to you.
1 Peter 1:25

APPENDIXES

BOOK OUTLINE

When I write, it helps me first to write my thoughts down as they come to me, without structure and order. Then I start to offer some design to my notes and begin to pen an outline of my thoughts.

As I thought about finishing this book, I decided to provide this outline as an appendix for my family to see how this book had developed. You will note that I didn't follow this outline too closely. Still, it has some merit to keep and share with you. But offer this in a 'hit-n-run' delivery format and not to further develop them into separate chapters. And because the following are quick notes, at places in the body of the book, I will contradict myself as prayer, research, and reflection bring the final position within the body of the book.

1   Selective Scripture verses
2   Copywrite Information
3   Dedication
4   Appreciation
5   Audience in mind – Purpose in writing
6   Introduction
    a. Third book of the series: The Sovereignty of God - to the return of Jesus - to life with Jesus.
    b. My wife Sandy – Personal Backgrounder
7   Field of Scriptures
8   Outline – RAW in format, still a work in progress.
    a. Brief description of creation
       i.   Earth – sin - mortality upon all creation from the garden – the hold of sin over the Earth
       ii. Heaven – The place where God currently lives

1. The Throne room of God
2. Many Rooms
3. The Kingdom of Heaven
4. The Fall of Satan – His access to God in Heaven today
   a. So if Satan is still allowed to be in Heaven, so then is there sin in Heaven too?
      i. Not from the saints who are in Christ in Heaven.
      ii. But from Satan and his angels
         1. For we do not wrestle against flesh and blood, but against the rulers, against the authorities, against the cosmic powers over this present darkness, **against the spiritual forces of evil in the Heavenly places. Ephesians 6:12**
         2. Now war arose in heaven, Michael and his angels fighting against the dragon. And the dragon and his angels fought back, but he was defeated, and there was no longer any place for them in heaven. And the great dragon was thrown down, that ancient serpent, who is called the devil and Satan, the deceiver of the whole world—he was thrown down to the earth, and his angels were thrown down with him. And I heard a loud voice in heaven, saying, "Now the salvation and the power and the kingdom of our God and the authority of his Christ have come, **for the accuser of our brothers has been thrown down, who accuses them day and night before our God**. And they have conquered him by the blood of the Lamb and by the word of their testimony, for they loved not their lives even unto

death. **Therefore, rejoice, O heavens and you who dwell in them!** Revelation 12:7-12a

5. For at the end of the age, there will be a new Heaven, Earth and Jerusalem that will be without sin.

   a. And the world is passing away along with its desires, but whoever does the will of God abides forever. 1 John 2:17

      i. **And when the thousand years are ended,** Satan will be released from his prison and will come out to deceive the nations that are at the four corners of the earth, Gog and Magog, to gather them for battle; their number is like the sand of the sea. **And they marched up over the broad plain of the earth and surrounded the camp of the saints** and the beloved city, but fire came down from heaven and consumed them, and the devil who had deceived them was thrown into the lake of fire and sulfur where the beast and the false prophet were, and they will be tormented day and night forever and ever. Revelation 20:7-10

      ii. Then I saw a new heaven and a new earth, **for the first heaven and the first earth had passed away, and the sea was no more.** And I saw the holy city, new Jerusalem, coming down out of heaven from God, prepared as a bride adorned for her husband. And I heard a loud voice from the throne saying, **"Behold, the dwelling place of God is with man.** He will dwell with them, and they will be his people, and God himself will be with them as their God. **He will [then?] wipe away every tear from their eyes,** and death shall be no more, neither shall there be mourning, nor crying, nor pain anymore, for the former things have passed away." Revelation 21:1-4

   iii. The Need for a Savior

     1. Jesus is the way, the truth and the life.

b. The power of the Holy Spirit in our lives - leading to the calling of our salvation while we are in our mortal bodies. Then, when a Christian dies, God moves us from life to life at our last breath – The Spirit is our Guarantee (physical body to spiritual body – and then to our resurrected bodies)

c. Question: Job says: And after my skin has been thus destroyed, yet in my flesh I shall see God, Job 19:26

   i. Are there three stages of bodies with flesh coverings?

     1. Flesh and Blood? Various [Mortal body]

     2. Flesh and spirit? Job 19:26 [Spiritual body?]

     3. Flesh and bones? "See my hands and my feet, that it is I myself. Touch me, and see. For a spirit does not have flesh and bones as you see that I have. Luke 24:39 [Immortal body]

   ii. Not sure. Maybe Job was referring to the time of his immortal body – Rapture and/or the first Resurrection?

   iii. Spiritual bodies are bodies. But will they have flesh as with what one is born?

     1. The disciples touched and ate with Jesus. Jesus rose into the clouds.

     2. When the apostles witnessed the transfiguration of Jesus, with Moses and Elijah in view … was Jesus in His Heavenly body or His Earthly body? What about Moses and Elijah?

a. It was His spiritual self that they saw
b. ¹ And after six days Jesus took with him Peter and James, and John his brother, and led them up a high mountain by themselves. ² And he was transfigured before them, and his face shone like the sun, and his clothes became white as light. ³ And behold, there appeared to them Moses and Elijah, talking with him. Matthew 17:1-3
d. Satan is the ruler of this world. And there is a time arriving in the future that he will cast from Heaven for good. And this must happen before the return of Jesus and the rapture.
e. God creates all humanity through His using man and woman through conception. Salvation comes to a man through God's saving grace through faith given to a man – through the power of the Holy Spirit, i.e., being Born Again - Born of the Spirit [John 3:6,8]. A man must be born again - first, by and through the working of the Holy Spirit, who testifies to our spirit that we are His.
   i. God creates all humanity through His using man and woman through conception. Salvation comes to a man through God's saving grace through faith given to a man – through the power of the Holy Spirit, i.e., being Born Again - Born of the Spirit [John 3:6,8]. A man must be born again - first, by and through the working of the Holy Spirit, who testifies to our spirit that we are His.
f. Three stages of life defined by Paul
   i. Mortal Body,
      1. As a Tent

a. For we know that if the tent that is our earthly home is destroyed, we have a building from God, a house not made with hands, eternal in the heavens. [2] For in this tent we groan, longing to put on our heavenly dwelling, 2 Corinthians 5:1-2

b. Physical Birth. Conceived in sin [iniquity]. Destined for the body to die and decay

   i. Wretched man that I am! Who will deliver me from this body of death? Romans 7:24

ii. Spiritual Body,

   1. Believers in Jesus prior to our time of physical death – having the Holy Spirit within in us - now at our last breath, receive our spiritual bodies through the Holy Spirit at death. This body is not as a tent but as a building – given from God

     a. **You yourselves like living stones are being built up as a spiritual house**, to be a holy priesthood, to offer spiritual sacrifices acceptable to God through Jesus Christ. 1 Peter 2:5

     b. Wearing white robes.

> After this I looked, and behold, a great multitude that no one could number, from every nation, from all tribes and peoples and languages, **standing before the throne and before the Lamb, clothed in white robes, with palm branches in their hands,**

washed their robes and made
them white in the blood of the
Lamb. Revelation 7:9-10

[Notice that they are standing
before the throne and before
Jesus - and they are clothed in
white robes, and have palm
branches with them – this is
during the Great Tribulation,
before Jesus' return back to Earth
and the Rapture]

c. So is it with the resurrection of the
dead. What is sown is perishable;
what is raised is imperishable. It is
sown in dishonor; it is raised in glory.
It is sown in weakness; it is raised in
power. It is sown a natural body; it is
raised a spiritual body. If there is a
natural body, there is also a spiritual
body. 1 Corinthians 15:42-44

2. Citizenship
a. **But our citizenship is in heaven, and
from it we await a Savior, the Lord
Jesus Christ, who will transform our
lowly body to be like his glorious
body,** by the power that enables him
even to subject all things to himself.
Therefore, my brothers, whom I love
and long for, my joy and crown, **stand
firm thus in the Lord**, my beloved.
Philippians 3:20 - 4:1

b. Please hold onto 'and from it.' For a
believer in Christ, having a physical

mortal body - at our last breath -He transitions us into spiritual bodies in Heaven – And from life in Heaven we await Jesus' return to complete our transformation into our resurrected bodies – to be just like Jesus!

iii. Resurrected Body.

   1. One unto righteousness – by/through the Holy Spirit. The Holy Spirit is our surety.

      a. He who has prepared us for this very thing is God, who has given us the Spirit as a guarantee. So we are always of good courage. We know that while we are at home in the body we are away from the Lord, [7] for we walk by faith, not by sight. 2 Corinthians 5:5-7

   2. Those outside of Christ - resurrected unto damnation for a life lived in unbelief in Jesus.

      a. Then the Lord knows how to rescue the godly from trials, and **to keep the unrighteous under punishment until the day of judgment,** and especially those who indulge in the lust of defiling passion and despise authority. 2 Peter 2:9-10

g. Three Locations presented to believers as stages of life today.

i. On Earth, mortal first, then

ii. In Heaven at death in our spiritual bodies, then

iii. Resurrected body leading to the New Earth and the New Jerusalem

h. Two stages of life at the second coming of Jesus for those alive on Earth when He does come - defined
   i. Mortal – Earthly then
   ii. Raptured
       1. For this we declare to you by a word from the Lord, that we who are alive, who are left until the coming of the Lord, will not precede those who have fallen asleep. For the Lord himself will descend from heaven with a cry of command, with the voice of an archangel, and with the sound of the trumpet of God. And the dead in Christ will rise first. Then we who are alive, who are left, will be caught up together with them in the clouds to meet the Lord in the air, and so we will always be with the Lord. Therefore encourage one another with these words.

       1 Thessalonians 4:15-18
       2. Leading to the new Earth, Heaven and Jerusalem
   iii. Please remember that the Holy Spirit is always within a believer, so as saved believers, He stays within us. Praise God!
i. What Life is like on …
   i. Earth,
       1. Corrupted.
           a. All men are sinful
           b. Only one man – Jesus is without sin
   ii. in Heaven,
       1. Mixture of Holiness and sin
           a. God, Jesus, The Spirit are perfect. All the saints who die in the promise of salvation through Jesus and are now in Heaven are in perfect holiness

through the works of Jesus, and the realm of Heavenly hosts that God has protected, are in perfect Holiness.

    i. And to the assembly of the firstborn who are enrolled in heaven, and to God, the judge of all, and to the spirits of the righteous made perfect, Hebrews 12:23

  b. Satan and his angels, until kicked out of Heaven by Michael and his army, are sin before the throne of God

iii. In the new Earth and new Jerusalem

  1. Sin is eradicated.

  2. Remembrance of the past are no longer.

    a. He will wipe away every tear from their eyes, and death shall be no more, neither shall there be mourning, nor crying, nor pain anymore, for the former things have passed away." Revelation 21:4

j. Will we be busy doing 'stuff?'

  i. [Move this reference]

k. In Heaven, is time measured?

  i. [1] When the Lamb opened the seventh seal, there was silence in heaven for about half an hour. Revelation 8:1;

  ii. And God called the expanse Heaven. And there was evening and there was morning, the second day. Genesis 1:8;

  iii. Making known to us the mystery of his will, according to his purpose, which he set forth in Christ [10] as a plan for the fullness of time, to unite all things in him, things in heaven and things on earth. Ephesians 1:9-10;

iv. And then the current Heaven and Earth will be no more, being replaced by new – implies a time future – which then is Prophecy fulfilled.

l. Remembering - Are we cognitive in Heaven to our life lived prior on Earth?

   i. Life,

   ii. Sorrow,

   iii. Joy

   iv. Good works

   v. Sin

   vi. Being part of the Cloud of witnesses- Can those who are with Jesus today have view to the accounts happening on the earth today?

       1. [1] Therefore, since **we are surrounded by so great a cloud of witnesses,** let us also lay aside every weight, and sin which clings so closely, and let us run with endurance the race that is set before us, [2] looking to Jesus, the founder and perfecter of our faith, who for the joy that was set before him endured the cross, despising the shame, and is seated at the right hand of the throne of God. **Hebrews 12:1-2**

       2. **Piper Reference:**

m. The Rapture Timing Conundrum

   i. When Jesus returns, the dead in Christ rise, and those who remain on the earth in Christ- meet Jesus and the saints in the air …

   ii. New physical bodies, right?

   iii. Rising up from the ground and sea – the saints – alive spiritually - dead physically, and those Christians who are alive on Earth – still within their mortal bodies - will meet with Jesus in the air. The Holy Spirit will conjoin the dead saints who now in their spiritual bodies given them when they died - with their new immortal bodies [mortal to spiritual to immortality]- with those who are alive are now transformed into their immortal bodies [mortal to immortality, noting that the Holy Spirit indwells all stages.

iv. Where then do those raptured saints go next after they meet in the air? [and I always wanted to fly without a plane]

1. It may depend on your eschatological view to the timing of the rapture.

    a. Do they stay in the clouds?

    b. Do they come back to Earth with Jesus right after?

    c. Or do they come back at another time?

    d. Do they return to Heaven and wait until God places the New Earth? Paul tells us that we have spiritual bodies when we die. He also tells us we will have immortal bodies when the rapture occurs. Could immortal physical bodies replace spiritual bodies in Heaven?

        i. Interject Dr. David Jeremiah, Moody Bible Position to question.

    e. [39] See my hands and my feet, that it is I myself. Touch me, and see. **For a spirit does not have flesh and bones as you see that I have."** [40] And when he had said this, he showed them his hands and his feet. [41] And while they still disbelieved for joy and were marveling, he said to them, "**Have you anything here to eat?**" [42] **They gave him a piece of broiled fish,** [43] **and he took it and ate before them.** Luke 24:39-43

f. Does Jesus return twice?

    i. Once for the rapture, and then a

    ii. Second time for judgement?

        1. View of Dr. David Jeremiah and other Pretribulationists.

g. OR - And just as it is appointed for man to die once, and after that comes judgment, so Christ, having been offered once to bear the sins of many, **will appear a second time, not to deal with sin but to save those who are eagerly waiting for him.** Hebrews 9:27-28

h. Then is the rapture and "the First Resurrection" the same event?

    i. **For as the Father raises the dead and gives them life, so also the Son gives life to those whom he will.** [The Father raises the dead and gives us spiritual life, when out tents fail, i.e. our Spiritual Body - 'For we know that if the tent that is our earthly home is destroyed, we have a building from God, a house not made with hands, eternal in the heavens. For in this tent we groan, longing to put on our heavenly dwelling, 2 Corinthians 5:1-2, Jesus then gives us our resurrected bodies when the Father sends Him back to earth, "We were buried therefore with him by baptism into death, in order that, just as Christ was raised from the dead by the glory of the Father, we too might walk in newness of life. For if we have been united with him in a death like his, we shall certainly be united with him in a resurrection like his. Romans 6:4-5] For the Father judges no one, but has given all judgment to the Son, that all may honor the Son, just as they honor the Father. Whoever does not honor the Son does not honor the Father who sent him. Truly, truly, I say to you, whoever hears my word and believes him who sent me has eternal life. He does not come into judgment, but has passed from death to life. "Truly, truly, I say to you, an hour is coming, and is now here, **when the dead will hear the voice of the Son of God, and those who hear will live**. For as the Father has life in himself, he has granted the Son also to have life in himself. And he has given him authority to execute judgment, because he is the Son of Man. Do not marvel at this, **for an hour is coming when all who are in the tombs** will hear his voice and come out, those who have done good to the resurrection of life, and those who have done evil to the resurrection of judgment.

John 5:21-29

ii. Then I saw thrones, and seated on them were those to whom the authority to judge was committed. **Also I saw the souls of those who had been beheaded for the testimony of Jesus and for the word of God, and those who had not worshiped the beast or its image and had not received its mark on their foreheads or their hands. They came to life and reigned with Christ for a thousand years.** Revelation 20:4

iii. The rest of the dead did not come to life until the thousand years were ended. This is the first resurrection. Revelation 20:5

iv. Something altogether different – unknown?

v. I lean to think that God will have various groups of saints given to various times of roles planned for each.

  1. The believers He has called prior to the rapture is one group.

  2. Those who die for their faith during the Great Tribulation.

3. Those who come to faith during God's Wrath may be another.
4. The Nation Israel yet another.
5. And those who were beheaded yet another group.
6. And what about those who are born in the New Earth era?
   a. [17] "For behold, I create
   new heavens
   and a new Earth, and
   the former things shall
   not be remembered
   or come into mind.
   [18] But be glad and
   rejoice forever
   in that which I create;
   for behold, I create
   Jerusalem to be a joy,
   and her people to be a
   gladness.
   [19] I will rejoice in
   Jerusalem
   and be glad in my
   people;
   no more shall be heard
   in it the sound of
   weeping
   and the cry of distress.
   [20] No more shall there
   be in it
   an infant who lives but
   a few days,
   or an old man who does

not fill out his days,
for the young man shall
die a hundred years old,
and the sinner a
hundred years old shall
be accursed.
²¹ They shall build
houses and inhabit
them;
they shall plant
vineyards and eat their
fruit.
²² They shall not build
and another inhabit;
they shall not plant and
another eat;
for like the days of a
tree shall the days of my
people be,
and my chosen shall
long enjoy the work of
their hands.
²³ They shall not labor
in vain
or bear children for
calamity,
for they shall be the
offspring of the blessed
of the LORD,
and their descendants
with them.
²⁴ Before they call I will
answer;
while they are yet
speaking I will hear.

²⁵ The wolf and the
lamb shall graze
together;
the lion shall eat straw
like the ox,
and dust shall be the
serpent's food.
They shall not hurt or
destroy
in all my holy
mountain,"
says the LORD. Isaiah
65:17-25

i.   So for those within the Rapture? I suggest when the call goes out when Jesus returns, we go wherever Jesus goes.

    i.   Then we who are alive, who are left, will be caught up together with them in the clouds to meet the Lord in the air, **and so we will always be with the Lord.** ¹⁸ Therefore encourage one another with these words. 1 Thessalonians 4:17-18

    ii.   And if I go and prepare a place for you, I will come again and **will take you to myself, that where I am you may be also** John 14:3

2.   It's important to understand that saints up until the rapture - experienced Jesus in four ways:

a.   Born - Mortal bodies.

b.   Born again- faith given by God sealed by the Holy Spirit as surety,

c. Spiritual Bodies – At our last breath,

d. Then Immortal [Raptured] Bodies – first fruits of the First Resurrection.

e. The timing between Mortal and Spiritual is easy to discern

f. The timing of the Spiritual to the Immortal body isn't as clearly revealed within scriptures to me, and I am taking into account all of scripture, but I position it is after the wrath of Satan and before the wrath of God..

n. Where do the dead who die in this life in unbelief in Jesus, where do they go at death?

    i. Hades – Site the rich man of Luke 16:19-31

o. When does the time of Judgement occur?

    i. Second Death.

p. Are we cognitively aware of our past in the new Heaven, new Earth and new Jerusalem too? Scripture points to a yes.

q. The witness of Paul to the third Heaven

r. The New Heaven and the New Earth

    i. Revelation 20-21

    ii. But according to his promise we are waiting **for new heavens and a new earth in which righteousness dwells.** 2 Peter 3:13

        1. For behold, I create new Heavens and a new Earth,
and the former things shall not be remembered
or come into mind. Isaiah 65:17

        2. "For as the new Heavens and the new Earth that I make
shall remain before me, says the LORD,

so shall your offspring and your name remain. Isaiah 66:22

   a.   Is this towards the saints or future, saved Israel?

9 Conclusion

10 So what about testimonies that people who died and went to Heaven and then medical folks "brought them back." Are these testimonies trust worthy?

   a.   And he heard things that cannot be told, which man may not utter. 2 Corinthians 12:4

   b.   Not like Paul, John, Ezekiel, Isaiah, for whom God gave them visions – but not as in dying and returning – [Might cut this section so as not to confuse]

11 Invitation

12 Indexes

13 About the Author

14 Back cover

PARKING LOT 01- THE RAPTURE

Research for Rapture Questions

My Research for The Pretribulation Two Returns of Jesus

[9] You, however, are not in the flesh but in the Spirit, if in fact the Spirit of God dwells in you. Anyone who does not have the Spirit of Christ does not belong to him. [10] But if Christ is in you, although the body is dead because of sin, the Spirit is life because of righteousness. [11] If the Spirit of him who raised Jesus from the dead dwells in you, he who raised Christ Jesus from the dead will also give life to your mortal bodies through his Spirit who dwells in you.

(Romans 8:9-11; emphasis added)

[29] "Immediately after the tribulation of those days the sun will be darkened, and the moon will not give its light, and the stars will fall from heaven, and the powers of the heavens will be shaken. [30] Then will appear in heaven the sign of the Son of Man, and then all the tribes of the earth will mourn, and *they will see the Son of Man coming on the clouds of heaven with power and great glory.* [31] And he will send out his angels with a loud trumpet call, and

they will gather his elect from the four winds, from one end of heaven to the other.

(Matthew 24:29-31; emphasis added)

[50] I tell you this, brothers: flesh and blood cannot inherit the kingdom of God, nor does the perishable inherit the imperishable. [51] Behold! I tell you a mystery. We shall not all sleep, but we shall all be changed, [52] in a moment, in the twinkling of an eye, **at the last trumpet**. For the trumpet will sound, and **the dead will be raised imperishable,**

[[3] Blessed be the God and Father of our Lord Jesus Christ! According to his great mercy, he has caused us to be born again to a living hope through the resurrection of Jesus Christ from the dead, [4] **to an inheritance that is imperishable, undefiled, and unfading, kept in heaven for you,** [5] who by God's power are being **guarded through faith for a salvation ready to be revealed in the last time.** (1 Peter 1:3-5; emphasis added)

[1] For we know that if the tent that is our earthly home is destroyed, we have a building from God, a house not made with hands, eternal in the heavens. [2] **For in this tent we groan, longing to put on our heavenly dwelling,** (spiritual body)[3] if indeed by putting it on we may not be found naked. [4] For while we are still in this tent, we groan, being burdened—not that we would be unclothed, but **that we would be further clothed, so that what**

is mortal may be swallowed up by life. [5] He who has prepared us for this very thing is God, who has given us the Spirit as a guarantee. (**2 Corinthians 5:1-5; emphasis added**)

and we shall be changed. [53] For this perishable body must put on the imperishable, and this mortal body must put on immortality [Physical Body]. [54] When the perishable puts on the imperishable, and the mortal puts on immortality, then shall come to pass the saying that is written: "Death is swallowed up in victory."[55] "O death, where is your victory? O death, where is your sting?"[56] The sting of death is sin, and the power of sin is the law. [57] But thanks be to God, who gives us the victory through our Lord Jesus Christ[58] Therefore, my beloved brothers, be steadfast, immovable, always abounding in the work of the Lord, knowing that in the Lord your labor is not in vain.

(1 Corinthians 15:50-58; emphasis added)

The Coming of the Lord

[13] But we do not want you to be uninformed, brothers, about those who are asleep, that you may not grieve as others do who have no hope. [14] For since we believe that Jesus died and rose again, even so, through Jesus, God will bring with him those who have fallen asleep. [15] For this we declare to you by a word from the Lord, that we who are alive, who are left until the coming of the Lord, will not precede those who have fallen asleep. [16] **For the Lord himself will descend from heaven with a cry of command, with the voice of an archangel, and with the sound of the trumpet of God**. And the dead in Christ will

rise first. [17] **Then we who are alive, who are left, will be caught up together with them in the clouds to meet the Lord in the air,** *and so we will always be with the Lord.* [18] Therefore encourage one another with these words.

(1 Thessalonians 4:13-18; emphasis added)

I say what I see scripture saying, we are with the Lord:

Then we who are alive, who are left, will be caught up together with them in the clouds to meet the Lord in the air, and so we will always be with the Lord. Therefore encourage one another with these words.

(1 Thessalonians 4:17-18)

So when Jesus returns, I can't say where we will be next after we meet Him in the clouds, except to say that we will always be with Jesus. I can say no more. I can say no less. But my heart says this happens at the end of the age. One day I am sure I'll find out.

Full Quote: Moody Bible Institute

https://www.moodybible.org/beliefs/
positional-statements/second-coming/

The Second Coming of Christ

We believe in the second coming of Christ. His return from heaven will be personal, visible and glorious, a blessed hope for which we should constantly watch and pray.[1]

Before He establishes His kingdom on earth, Jesus will come for His Church, an event commonly referred to as the "Rapture." At that time the dead in Christ will be raised and living Christians will be caught up to meet the Lord in the air and be with Him forever.[2] In this resurrection, those who have died in Christ will have their redeemed souls and spirits united with a body similar to Christ's glorified body. Christians living at the time of this event will not die, but will be changed to be like Christ.[3] This expectation is a motivation for holy living, as well as a source of comfort.[4] No man knows the day or the hour when this will take place.[5]

After the Rapture of the Church, Christians will be brought before the judgment seat of Christ. He will reward them on the basis of the works they have accomplished.[6] This is not a judgment to determine their salvation but a reward for labor on Christ's behalf.[7] The Rapture will also inaugurate a period that the Bible characterizes as the "great day of His wrath," "the great tribulation" and the "time of Jacob's trouble." This time of unprecedented difficulty will affect Israel and all nations. Its purpose will be to prepare Israel for her Messiah.[9]

At the end of the Tribulation, Jesus Christ will return with the hosts of heaven as well as the Church to establish the Messianic Kingdom on earth.[10] His Kingdom will last for a thousand years.[11] At this Second Coming, the Antichrist will be cast into the Lake of Fire and Satan will be bound for a thousand years [12] The nations and their representatives will be judged.[13] Israel will be restored to her land, never more to be removed.[14] Christ will reign with firmness and equity.[15] His kingdom will be marked by material and spiritual blessing, since the curse upon the earth will be removed.[16]

The Messianic kingdom will close with apostasy and rebellion.[17] God will crush this uprising in the last battle of the ages and Satan will be thrown into the lake of fire.[18] All those who rejected the Word of God will be resurrected.[19] They will be judged by Christ and cast into the lake of fire, the place where they will suffer final and everlasting punishment.[20]

After this judgment there will be a new heaven and a new earth, where righteousness is the norm.[21] There will be a new Jerusalem and the everlasting presence of God among all the redeemed.[22]

[1] Zechariah 14:4; Acts 1:11; Titus 2:13; Revelation 1:7
[2] 1 Corinthians 15:51–54; 1 Thessalonians 4:14
[3] 1 John 3:2
[4] 1 John 2:28; 1 Thessalonians 4:18
[5] Matt. 24:36; John 6:39
[6] Romans 14:10–12; 2 Corinthians 5:10
[7] 1 Corinthians 3:9–15
[8] Revelation 6:17; 7:14; Jeremiah 30:7
[9] Zechariah 12:2, 3; 14:1–3
[10] Revelation 19:7–9, 14; 1 Thessalonians 3:13; Zechariah 14:9; Revelation 19:15, 16
[11] Revelation 20:2, 4–6
[12] Revelation 19:20; 20:1–3
[13] Joel 3; Matthew 25
[14] Amos 9:15; Ezekiel 34:28
[15] Psalms 2:9; Isaiah 11:4
[16] Romans 8:19-21
[17] Revelation 20:7–9
[18] Revelation 20:10
[19] Revelation 20:11–13
[20] Revelation 20:14, 15; Mark 9:48
[21] 2 Peter 3:13
[22] Revelation 21:2, 3; 2:3–5

END MOODY BIBLE INSTITUTE QUOTE

Billy Graham Evangelistic Association: What is the Rapture

https://billygraham.org/answer/what-is-the-rapture/
Q: What is the rapture?

A: There are many Christians who believe that the second coming of Jesus Christ will be in two phases. First, He will come for believers, both living and dead, in the "rapture" (read 1 Thessalonians 4:13-17). In this view, the rapture—which is the transformation and catching up of all Christians, dead or alive, to meet Christ in the air—will be secret, for it will be unknown to the world of unbelievers at the time of its happening.

The effect of this removal, in the absence of multitudes of people, will, of course, be evident on earth. Then, second, after a period of seven years of tribulation on earth, Christ will return to the earth with His church, the saints who were raptured (Matthew 24:30, 2 Thessalonians 1:7, 1 Peter 1:13, Revelation 1:7). He will be victorious over His enemies and will reign on the earth for 1,000 years (the millennium) with His saints, the church.

After 1,000 years, living unbelievers and the wicked dead now raised to life will be judged at the great white throne judgment. They will then be cast into the lake of fire, while the saved will live forever with Christ in a new heaven and earth (Revelation, chapters 19-22).

Many other evangelical Christians believe that Christ's return and the rapture will not occur until the seven years of the tribulation have ended. As far as the latter view is concerned, the rapture will not be secret, since it will be part of Christ's visible and triumphant return to end this present evil age (1 Thessalonians 4:13-17). At this point, interpreters differ as to whether there will be a literal thousand-year reign of Christ on earth or whether the white throne judgment and the new heaven and earth will immediately appear.

All Christians do not agree on every detail of what will occur in the final events of this world's history. Some of these events and their order of occurrence have simply not been made clear in the Bible. What is important is that all Christians hold in common that Christ will ultimately return bodily, visibly, and gloriously to reign and rule with His resurrected and transformed saints forever and ever. The details of this great event will be made known in God's own time.

Robert Van Kampen: The Sign – The Rapture

"When "the dead in Christ" are raised, this group will include, in this writer's opinion [Robert Van Kampen], the Old Testament saints as well as the New. A number of Old Testament passages give a prophetic preview of the Rapture of these Old Testament saints, paralleling the same timing given in the New Testament for the true church of Christ. For example, the Lord inspired Isaiah to write,

> [19] Your dead shall live; their bodies shall rise.
> You who dwell in the dust, awake and sing for joy!
> For your dew is a dew of light,
> and the earth will give birth to the dead.
> [20] Come, my people, enter your

chambers,
and shut your doors behind you;
hide yourselves for a little while
until the fury has passed by.
[21] For behold, the LORD is coming out
from his place
to punish the inhabitants of the earth
for their iniquity,
and the earth will disclose the blood
shed on it,
and will no more cover its slain. Isaiah
26:19-21

Remarkable, this ancient passage seems to speak specifically about the Rapture as it relates to certain other events that occur during the end times. Thus verse 19 describes the resurrection of all the believing dead; verse 20 gives a warning to "my people," that in the end times they will have to hide from the Antichrist until rescued by the Lord; and verse 21 tells of the Day-of-the-Lord wrath that immediately follows—which is the exact sequence of events developed in chapters 16 and 17 of this book." **Robert Van Kampen "The Sign of Christ's Coming and the End of the Age:, Page 339**

PARKING LOT 02 –
THE BRIDE OF CHRIST

Research for the Bride of Christ

So is the Church the Bride of Jesus?

In my final book edit, I cut the following section from Chapter Ten to contain the focus and not introduce another sidebar. However, instead of discarding it, I decided to keep it as backup material as further reference in support that the Bride is not the Church, but she is saved Israel.

Ephesians 5:25-27 revisited.

So then I had to go back and relook at Ephesians 5:25-27.

> Husbands, love your wives, as Christ loved the church and gave himself up for her, that he might sanctify her, having cleansed her by the washing of water with the word, so that he might present the church to himself in splendor, without spot or wrinkle or any such thing, that she might be holy and without blemish.
>
> (Ephesians 5:25-27)

Does Paul say that the church is the bride of Jesus? Or is Paul saying that Christ and the church are connected as a husband, and his wife is connected?

Jesus set up the church. Jesus sets the church apart. Jesus calls the church in the feminine gender as to be like a bride. And yes, Jesus cleanses her [the church] through His word, so that Jesus presents the church to Himself, and that the church would be holy, without spot, wrinkle or blemish. This position is where I was before.

But I now also see Paul using this to support his previous statements:

> For the husband is the head of the wife even as Christ is the head of the church, his body, **and is himself its Savior**. Now as the church submits to Christ, so also wives should submit in everything to their husbands.

> (Ephesians 5:23-24)

After closer inspection, Paul gives us this 'metaphor' of the marriage union between a husband and wife and Jesus and the Church. As the Church is the body of Christ, my heart says that being IN Christ is more profound than being the bride. So as a wife takes instruction to submit to her husband, the Church is to do the same.

> For no one ever hated his own flesh, but nourishes and cherishes it, just as Christ does the church, because **we are members of his body**. "Therefore a man shall leave his father and mother and hold fast to his wife, and the two shall become one flesh." This mystery is profound, and I am saying that it refers to Christ and the church.

> (Ephesians 5:29-32; emphasis added)

Paul now goes deeper! "No one ever hated his own flesh!" Hmmm. What does Paul mean? This statement isn't about being Jesus' bride, but "because we are members of His body." In salvation, Jesus lives within us by His Spirit! Forever! Not to the anticipation of a future wedding. So I ask again, is the Church the Bride of Christ?

All right then, What About 2 Corinthians 11:2?

Let's take a look.

> I wish you would bear with me in a little foolishness.
> Do bear with me! <u>For I feel a divine jealousy for you,</u>
> <u>since I betrothed you to one husband, to present you as a</u>
> <u>pure virgin to Christ.</u> But I am afraid that as the serpent
> deceived Eve by his cunning, your thoughts will be led
> astray from a sincere and pure devotion to Christ. For if
> someone comes and proclaims another Jesus than the one
> we proclaimed, or if you receive a different spirit from the
> one you received, or if you accept a different gospel from
> the one you accepted, you put up with it readily enough.
> Indeed, I consider that I am not in the least inferior to
> these super-apostles. Even if I am unskilled in speaking,
> I am not so in knowledge; indeed, in every way we have
> made this plain to you in all things.
>
> (2 Corinthians 11:1-6; emphasis added)

I have to admit it. If you scan this, it does indicate marriage to Christ. But if
we look closer, it supports more the body of Christ than the bride of Christ.

The church at Corinth was a wild church; for they needed correction from
Paul on many subjects as to what true faith is. And Paul goes to great
lengths to position himself and his God-given authority before chapter
eleven. For Paul felt pushback - he still needed to set his ministry within
this church by supposing that they might oppose him, thus giving his
defense. Thus, Paul goes to great lengths to build his defense, hoping they
would understand his counsel through the Spirit of Christ.

> For we are not overextending ourselves, as though we
> did not reach you. For we were the first to come all the
> way to you with the gospel of Christ. We do not boast

beyond limit in the labors of others. But our hope is that as your faith increases, our area of influence among you may be greatly enlarged, so that we may preach the gospel in lands beyond you, without boasting of work already done in another's area of influence. "Let the one who boasts, boast in the Lord."

(2 Corinthians 10:14-17; emphasis added)

Therefore, Paul says, 'bear with me as I present to you a little foolishness,' an absurd example of what true faith looks like to make his point.

'If it were up to me to present you as a wife to Jesus, I'd want you to be pure. As a virgin,' Paul says, 'but as the devil deceived Eve, so are you.'

I see this not as the Corinthian church as the bride of Jesus, or even by application, fitting every church. But to the church in Corinth - for them to shape up! If this church had true faith in Christ, they wouldn't have fallen into deception when another 'savior' came along. This writing of Paul's to this church is Paul's instruction and not his declaration to the Corinthians that they are betrothed to Jesus. Paul says, 'clean up your act and know the basis of your salvation if indeed you are truly saved.'

Jews for Jesus Statement of Faith: Israel

https://jewsforjesus.org/about/statement-of-faith Pulled 1/22/22.

We believe that Israel exists as a covenant people through whom God continues to accomplish His purposes and that the Church is an elect people in accordance with the New Covenant, comprising both Jews and Gentiles who acknowledge Jesus as Messiah and Redeemer. We believe that Jesus the Messiah will return personally in order to consummate the prophesied purposes concerning His kingdom.

The International Christian Embassy Jerusalem:

"This moment of inspection of the wedding garments is very instructive! The Fall festivals – Rosh Hashana, Yom Kippur and Feast of Tabernacles – are all tied together and all portend the Second Coming of Jesus! They speak prophetically of the Coronation of Jesus as King and the Wedding Feast of the Lamb.

The Parable of the Wedding Feast assumes the listener is familiar with the ancient Oriental custom of the host providing garments for the guests who were invited to a royal feast. In ancient times, kings and wealthy men had wardrobes filled with fancy garments (today called 'caftans') as a symbol of their wealth and glory. Examples can be found as follows:

Genesis 45:22 – Joseph gives all his brother garments, but three garments to Benjamin.

Judges 14:12 – Samson offers 30 linen garments and 30 changes of clothes to answer his riddle.

2 Kings 5:22 – Naaman promises 10 garments plus gold and silver to Elisha.

2 Kings 10:22 – King Jehu gives vestments from wardrobe in the temple of Baal.

Esther 6:8 and 8:15 – Haman says: "dress him in royal robes" / Mordechai is the one dressed in royal apparel.

Even today, at very posh country clubs and restaurants, there are similar strict dress codes, and small closets with appropriate dinner jackets and other attire if an improperly dressed guest warrants entry.

In the parable of Jesus, it would have been a great insult to the king to refuse to wear the garments freely offered to the guests. The man who was caught wearing his old clothing learned what an offense it was as he was forcefully removed from the celebration.

This was Jesus' way of teaching the inadequacy of self-righteousness. From the very beginning, God provided a "covering" for our sin. Adam and Eve tried to cover their nakedness and shame with fig leaves, but God replaced them with skins of animals, which meant a life had been sacrificed (Genesis 3:7, 21). To insist on covering our shame ourselves is to be clad in "filthy rags" (Isaiah 64:6). In the book of Revelation, we see those in heaven wearing "white robes" (Revelation 7:9), and we learn that the whiteness of the robes is due to their being washed in the blood of the Lamb (verse 14). We trust in God's righteousness, not our own (Philippians 3:9). Further, the true Church is described as "not having spot, or wrinkle" (Ephesians 5:27).

Finally, in Revelation 19:6-9, a great multitude has gathered for the "marriage of the Lamb ... and His wife has made herself ready. And to her it was granted to be arrayed in fine linen, clean and bright, for the fine linen is the righteous acts of the saints. Then he said to me, "Write: 'Blessed are those who are called to the marriage supper of the Lamb!'"" [*Yom Kippur: A Day to Prepare our Wedding Garments*, International Christian Embassy Jerusalem: Pulled 04-22-2022 https://int.icej.org/news/headlines/yom-kippur-day-prepare-our-wedding-garments,]

PARKING LOT 03 – OTHER QUESTIONS

Questions that didn't make the cut or fit well into the central body of work.

For I didn't have solid Bible-based answers to share, just my thoughts.

However, my questions are my questions. Maybe some of these are yours as well?

And remember, "But, as it is written, 'What no eye has seen, nor ear heard, nor the heart of man imagined, what God has prepared for those who love him'" 1 Corinthians 2:9.

Question. If there are rooms, houses, cities, and places in Heaven, i.e., Heavenly places, will Heaven also have dirt and vegetation like Earth?

My Opinion. The Bible is silent on this. God created the Earth for the physical; Jesus came as a man, born into the World. So I would say that seeing God has a purpose in living eternally in the physical realm, ruling and reigning from the New Earth one day - again in His physically resurrected body. Heaven is the spiritual realm of life. We know God's house has rooms, and the inhabitants wear robes. And God sits on His throne, so possibly furniture. But scripture doesn't share if there is dirt, grass, or vegetation; for we live and walk by the Spirit. Thus the Earth and the galaxies have a physical matter, with Earth having soil and vegetation. But, again, my speculation is in logic, not my teaching from the Bible. Oh, what wonders that will be revealed to us on the day of our last breath.

Question. Asked differently, will there be fields and meadows between Heavenly places?

My Opinion. No. Only on Earth, as Genesis One declares, has vegetation.

Question. The Bible presents a visual description of God's throne room, as testified by the prophets and disciples as they wrote. Is what they experienced unique to only the throne room?

My Opinion. The Bible is silent to describe anything more than what we read about the throne room of God. Within chapter Seven, I ask about the furnishing of 'our rooms.' But as you may recall, I don't have a good answer to that question either.

Question. All the saints will have white robes. So I wonder, who makes our robes? Or how do we receive the robes?

My Opinion. Pure speculation on my part; but I think we will be presented with our robes the instant of our last breath. Knowing that we will be 'clothed in Jesus' righteousness,' wearing white robes will signify that we are appropriately attired, wearing our wedding garments. Not a wedding gown – for I positioned that saved Israel is the Bride. We receive our robes [the wedding garment - **robes of Christ's righteousness**] the instant we receive our spiritual bodies. But who makes our robes? Ultimately God has created all things, so maybe God is. I am reminded in Genesis 3 that when Adam and Eve first sinned, Jesus killed the animals to make clothes for them. So why not also having prepared the robes of His righteousness for our arrival into Heaven?

Question. Will there be a need for a clothes closet?

My Opinion. Because of sin, we have dust, pollen, dirt, and germs on Earth. And as such, things need to be cleaned and refreshed. However, I mean that one robe will be enough to wear and will never need to be cleaned, pressed, altered, or changed. I also envision that since eating is a physical characteristic of life on Earth, we won't spill juice on ourselves in Heaven. [Your favorite smiley emoji goes here.]

Question. Will we have access to roam the kingdom?

My Opinion. I would believe so. As we travel and gaze at all God has created for His glory to be displayed here in this World, I would imagine it to be 1000% greater within the realm of Heaven. But remember, this is weak speculation on my part. Many of my comments are from my life experiences on this Earth. The characteristics of being human as God has created, and being part of the body of Christ, as He also determined, are beyond my comprehension, or what I can imagine is in Heaven. Thus, this is why these questions are not within the main body of work of the book. And life on Earth is just the beginning of seeing the wonder and the glory of our Lord and Savior.

Question. What about access to the stars, planets, and galaxies?

My Opinion. I don't think so. My first impression is no, for the creation of the physical is a testimony to the glory of God before fallen humanity. For that which is physical - is physical, and that which is spiritual is spiritual. Therefore, in the beginning, God created all things to surround His creation of the World – Earth.

Genesis 1:14-15

> And God said, "Let there be lights in the expanse of the heavens to separate the day from the night. And let them be for signs and for seasons, and for days and years, and let them be lights in the expanse of the heavens to give light upon the Earth." And it was so.

Question. And if we do, will we travel or instantly appear there?

My Opinion. God is everywhere and at all times and in all places. First, as I stated above, the physical is to humanity to see the Glory of God in creation. Thus I would think, just as with Earth, the saints in Heaven can see but cannot visit. Refer back to the great cloud of witnesses section in Chapter Seven. I share that the Heavenly saints are in Heaven until the rapture, for they have a view but not the ability to be on this Earth, except when God called for Moses and Elijah back to Earth to participate in Jesus' transfiguration before the disciples. And then to the future time, when the two witnesses come down from Heaven to testify to the world, the need for repentance and faith in Jesus is required.

Question. We all will have roles given to us; as an example, the disciples will judge the 12 tribes of Israel in New Jerusalem. Will all the rest of the saints have authority roles, too? Or will some of the saints just be assigned tasks of a lesser degree?

My Opinion. I don't know.

Question. Which leads to a hierarchy of positions. There are various degrees of talents that Jesus shares about the faithful servants. Thus, may I suggest that there is a hierarchical position within Heaven? The throne room of God has Elders and angels that have unique roles. We will all have our roles and functions given to us by God.

My Opinion. I believe so. The Body of Christ is not made up of all arms or legs here on this Earth. But each member is different and serves a specific function. My heart says that living in Heaven and the New Earth - will be no different.

Question. When the rapture happens, what happens after we meet in the clouds? We are always with Jesus, but where do we all go next?

My Opinion: To Earth with Jesus. But as to where, I don't know. Some say the Mount Of Olives. Others declare we stay in the clouds. So I state that we are always with Jesus, as 1 Thessalonians 4:17 reports.

PARKING LOT 04 – MOURNING THE LOSS OF A LOVED ONE.

I am writing this section as the last section of my book and my closing words in finishing this book. As I write, it is approaching ten months since my wife passed.

When I first began this endeavor, in reflection, my heart was tender in missing my beloved. My writing helped me work through the pain of loss—the quiet of home, and missing my best friend.

Now know that as I finish the book, the pain, the silence, and the missing haven't gone away, but have greatly diminished. So some folks may want to know, to be comforted, or to understand how life is today for me. At the moment of now. Now that it's almost a year.

Living today without the one you deeply loved for a long time, and now without them, you may want to know if there is real and experienced hope. I declare a resounding YES. But know that this experience stays with you to various degrees in my daily life.

Some days all joy besets my thoughts, knowing that Sandy is with Jesus! One day I will be too.

Then, a trigger will touch my heart of remembrance, and a moment of sadness will burst into my heart. It may be a shared experience I am now doing by myself. Or a turned phrase between us that I heard in a conversation at church or the store. It creeps in, unaware that it triggers a fond memory, and it shifts my mood to relive the loss of her - all of a sudden. But what I choose to do next can make the difference between a good day and a bad one. And for me, my go-to place, my solace, is prayer and the word of God.

I have to look ahead, not behind, for the car's windshield is much larger than the rearview mirror. I must remember to enter what is before me, not what is past, which I have departed.

Oh, the days will still come, and I imagine, even year over year, if God grants me more years in my life path. For I must choose to see the bigger picture, that life is about Christ and not about my wife. And not about me. Through our faith in and through Jesus, Sandy and I have enjoyed a blessed marriage. We always stated, 'Jesus comes first. You are next - me last.'

I can tell you that many Earthly behaviors have changed, and I am living in my new normal. I have learned to do many new tasks. Of these tasks, I have become good at accomplishing them. And some new roles, I would give myself a passing grade. But life moves forward.

My love for my wife will never go away; for God blessed me with her, and in my heart, she will always be remembered and loved fondly. As I wrote, I pray I have the room in God's house next to hers.

But one has to know that Jesus is more important than anything or anyone else. And it would help if you didn't misunderstand what I am sharing. Marriage is a blessing in this life, but it is temporary. And we need to accept this as God has granted it to us.

Grief moved me to mourn for my loss of her moved faster than I expected. And then fond remembering appreciation and praise to God for our season of time together also came quickly.

I praise God for the Holy Spirit and the people He sent to my family and me to provide the prayers, comfort, and support we needed. LOVE covers everything, and the love of Christ filled my heart during the early and challenging times of the first few months.

My advice to those in Christ when someone you know has lost a loved one is to love upon them. Call them and pray for and with them. Visit with them. Just be there for them.

And to those who may have just lost a loved one, remember, your life doesn't stop. It has just changed. It starts hard because it is a dramatic change in our lives. But seek and run to Jesus, for He is there to direct your steps.

Renew your mind by reading your bible. The Psalms are perfect for comfort if you need a starting point. And don't mourn too long. Pray that God will change your heart to continue to seek the joy of your salvation in Christ. And that your loss is Christ's gain as your loved one is now with Him.

Having been faithful to Sandy throughout our marriage by the grace of God, it is a bit hard to imagine being married again. God kept my eyes from the temptation of lust, for Sandy was the best for me. But for being married again, I'm learning to lean more on what Jesus wants of me than I want of Him. With Sandy, I so enjoyed being married to her. Not of receiving, but of giving.

In a casual comment a few years ago at a bible study, Sandy stated that I needed to be married again if she would pass first, which confirms that she knew how much I loved her. What joy in this sinful world I had in having a Christian, god-placed woman as my wife and best friend for forty years. So my prayer for today is, 'God, you know best; whatever you have planned is best for me.'

No one can replace our wives or husbands. But if God calls for another, there is a reason and purpose, for they are an additive, not a substitute or surrogate.

God has a plan and a purpose in life. Paul declares: "And we know that for those who love God all things work together for good, for those who are called according to his purpose." Romans 8:28

So count it all joy as soon as you can. Know that there will still be triggers in your heart that will bring a moment of sadness to missing your loved one. And know that life on this Earth is the stepping stone into eternity with Jesus, the author, finisher, and perfector of our faith.

God gave Sandy a life path that included being my wife and the mother of our children, raising and preparing them for their kingdom work. Her mission is now complete, and she is before Jesus in reward.

Our mission path is still before us. Let's continue to walk in faith, doing the works of an evangelist until we are called home or Christ is called to return for us!

To God be the glory!

ABOUT THE AUTHOR

In life, each day is a gift from God. And throughout life, He also blesses us with things expected and unexpected. I have been so blessed, more than I can write. For, outside of my salvation in Jesus, my wife Sandy is right behind the blessings of salvation - in having a Christian woman as my wife and life partner. And from there, my kids and my grandkids are also my blessings and treasures in life.

This picture of Sandy is from our wedding day on January 29, 1982. I share this as a small tribute to Christ's love for us. And I present this as my remembrance of her.

It's hard to order all that Jesus has done, but to say that I am so blessed to have the family He has given me, and that they, too, are in Christ brings me to my knees in gratitude with thanksgiving.

Having just finished my second book about the signs of Jesus' return and the end of this age – *En Route to the Mount of Olives* – *Matthew 24*. I felt the calling to author this book next. I humbly praise God for the honor and privilege of doing so.

I pray that He will have me continue to write about Him as my life starts in the next chapter. And I pray that He would help me endure as a witness and testimony of His loving grace and mercy to my family, friends, and you, the reader.

As Psalms 139:16 declares: "Your eyes saw my unformed substance; in your book were written, every one of them, the days that were formed for me, when as yet there was none of them."

So my ask of you is to pray for God's glory. Pray that He continues to change your and my hearts to be more conformed to the image of Jesus. And pray that He will keep us both in the faith of, in, and through Jesus. And pray that God will continue to use me to write about His glory for my family, friends, and you as long as He grants me the days.

In Jesus' name, and for and to His glory, Amen!

OTHER BOOKS BY DAVID ROSEN

The Sovereignty of God in Our Daily Lives, 2021

Christian Faith Publishing, 832 Park Avenue, Meadville, PA 16335

ISBN: 978-1-63874-188-6 Paperback

ISBN: 978-1-638-74-189-3 Digital

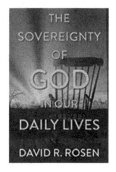

This book is about the sovereignty of God. I am writing specifically toward those who believe, with an eye toward those who are drawn seeking. The Gospel of Christ, through seeing God's sovereignty in our salvation - and now also within our lives, should help the reader see the glory of Christ in our daily walk of faith. Salvation is not a one-time event, and my challenge is not solely because of your or my efforts. For it is a gift of grace through faith by God; for beneath our faith in Jesus is God's active working within our hearts. Now, with the Holy Spirit living within us, He works daily in us, to the council of His will, toward, in, and through us-giving us His grace, wisdom, and comfort each day.

This book, with the Bible in hand, highlights scriptures with my comments as a flashlight, highlights the glory of God and to help reveal to believers and seekers alike the high value of Jesus!

En Route to The Mount of Olives – Matthew 24, 2022

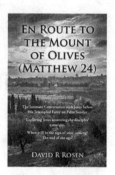

Christian Faith Publishing, 832 Park Avenue,
Meadville, PA 16335

ISBN: 978-1-68570-845-0 Paperback

ISBN: 978-1-68570-846-7 Digital

And now - it is time. And as God has arranged and prepared. As the scriptures have been foretold - for the crucifixion of Jesus is now but days away! Jesus had been preparing His disciples for the time of this week. And now, we jump into the Word. Jesus and His disciples are now leaving the Temple. And they are heading across the way up toward the Mount of Olives. For the time of Jesus' last Passover observance with His Disciples is before Him. And then, He transforms His last Passover with His Disciples into The Last Supper [Matthew 26:17-19].

So picture yourself standing in the courtyard - in view is the Mount of Olives. Jesus has just finished rebuking the Scribes and Pharisees in his telling the crowds and disciples the seven woes of their hypocritical faith [as recorded within Matthew 23], and now Jesus and His disciples are preparing to leave the courtyard, and you overhear the disciples' note to Jesus the splendor of the Temple

And in return reply, Jesus offers an unexpected comment - actually, Jesus offers a prophecy that He presents back to them – "But he answered them, 'You see all these, do you not? Truly, I say to you, there will not be left here one stone upon another that will not be thrown down.'" [Matthew 24:2]. And now, the journey to cross over from the temple courtyard to the Mount of Olives begins.

Printed in the United States
by Baker & Taylor Publisher Services